Plains Indian Mythology

BY THE AUTHORS

American Indian Mythology
Peyote
Plains Indian Mythology

Plains Indian Mythology

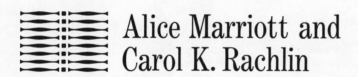 Alice Marriott and
Carol K. Rachlin

Thomas Y. Crowell Company
NEW YORK / ESTABLISHED 1834

All photographs by Carol K. Rachlin unless otherwise noted.

Library of Congress Cataloging in Publication Data

Marriott, Alice Lee
    Plains Indian mythology.

    Bibliography: p.
    1. Indians of North America—Great Plains—Religion and mythology. 2. Indians of North America—Great Plains—Legends. I. Rachlin, Carol K., joint author. II. Title.
E78.G73M37 1975   299'.7   75-26554
ISBN 0-690-00694-2

10   9   8   7   6   5   4   3   2   1

*For all the tellers of tales who
are gone, and for their grandchildren,
who are still with us*

Acknowledgments

Our gratitudes are many. To Dr. Donald Humphery, Philbrook Art Museum, Tulsa, Oklahoma, to Gillette Griswold of the United States Army Field Artillery and Fort Sill Museum, Fort Sill, Oklahoma, to Arminta Neal of the Denver Museum of Natural History, to Richard Conn of the Denver Art Museum, and to Norman Paulson of the State Historical Society of North Dakota for photographic materials. Our thanks go to our friends and informants and interpreters, named and unnamed, who brought this book about. And to our colleagues and students at Central State University, Edmond, Oklahoma, who have made time for research and writing available to us. Our appreciation and thanks to Lawana Kent Brown who helped in so many ways. And finally who can ever fail to thank Dr. Benjamin Botkin, of Croton-on-the-Hudson, New York, for helping found the school and method of American folklore as we know it today?

Contents

Photographs

Foreword

The themes of myths have been the preoccupation of folklorists for the last two centuries. To trace an elusive plan or plot to its place of origin, to relate it to other stories having similar meanings or components, has been the great preoccupation of scholars since Charles Perrault and the Brothers Grimm discovered the diffusion of the Cinderella story throughout northern Europe.

Seldom has the real meaning of the word "folklore" actually been analyzed and examined. The lore of the folk has often been ignored in favor of such themes as the Primeval Flood, the bringing—or catching—of the Sun, the creation of life, and the opposite theme, the coming of death.

Probably George Washington Cable and Mark Twain were the first to perceive that the *telling* of a tale, as opposed to its principal subject matter, was as significant as the story itself. This attitude was enlarged upon in the first quarter of the twentieth century by such Texans as J. Frank Dobie and Mody C. Boatright, and by Ben Botkin and his students and co-workers in Oklahoma. Preoccupation with themes there will always be, of course. But the why and the how of the telling, the choice of words and their combinations, the incidental cultural information contained within the story itself went largely unheeded by most folklorists.

It is another matter for consideration that the earliest recorders of folktales of the American Indians were scholarly linguists, concerned more with the preservation of vanishing languages than with subject matter. Franz Boas, who more nearly than anyone else represented the complete anthropologist, was so concerned with words that he often translated passages that were perfectly proper in Kwakiutl but utterly obscene in English, into Latin. Since Latin was a dying language even in Boas's day, and has since vanished into limbo even in the Roman Catholic Mass, there are few specialists in folklore who can today read Boas's interpolations. Also, the writing style current at any given time must be considered. Hiawatha is an interesting example of Victorian poetry, but any relationship it bears to American Indian mythology is purely coincidental.

True it is that every anthropologist is at the mercy of his interpreters. The word omitted, the meaning slurred, the substitution of a synonym, are inevitable. Half a century ago this was not so serious a matter. Interpreters could be found who were literate in English, and in good English. Today, good English, like Latin, seems to be vanishing into oblivion for Indians and non-Indians alike. The use of the precise word, the concept of language as a tool which must be kept sharpened, has perished beneath the heels of mass communication and permissive parenthood.

There is a greater gap between the teacher who has learned English as a worthy means of expression in itself and the student who has never thought of it as anything but a nuisance than there is between speakers of unrelated languages, for languages *can be taught and learned.* So can one's native language, but there are few who are interested in the subtleties, especially if the language happens to be English.

The great artistic expression of American Indians was verbal, even oral, and much of its literature has been lost. There are many reasons for this. Perhaps the primary is that Indian languages, like European languages, have changed over a period of time. We are better able to understand Chaucerian English than some Indian groups are able to understand their ceremonial or old language. Many Indians cannot speak their own language, and still others have very limited vocabularies in their native tongue. Many Indians were removed to Indian boarding schools at an early age and never heard the ancient stories and ceremonies recited by the old people. And many Indians simply were not interested in the old ways and never learned them. Thus, much became lost and much became fragmented when a generation died.

We have come to the place where it seems advisable to pause and redefine our terms. *Mythology* is the backbone of religion; the accounts of the supernatural, superhuman beings who have become embodied in the universe: Sun, Moon, Stars, Winds, and the Earth herself.

Legendry falls into two sections: the how and why, or explanatory stories, such as are told questioning children, and the accounts of men and women who actually have lived, but who, since their lifetimes, have become larger than life. Such men in our own culture, as George Washington and Benjamin Franklin, carry with them an aura of legend because they have been gone from us many years.

There is a third category of storytelling: *folklore*. These stories are literally the lore and the wisdom of the folk. They are as old as time and as new as tomorrow. They are told of ordinary people in extraordinary circumstances; they may be based on personal experience, or on something heard from others.

We have included all three—myth, legend, and folklore—in this collection. The myths are old and so are some of the how and why stories. The legends are newer, but that is to be expected, as Plains Indian life has gone through so many changes in the past two centuries. We have included personal folklore and the words to some of the modern Plains Indian songs. We feel that the modern is as important as the old myths; legends and folklore are always being made.

We have chosen to present the material in this book as a continuum; not as a formal mythology per se. It is Indian, beginning with the days of the very beginnings, as told by Indians themselves to us in English. If the emphasis seems to be more on the tribes of the southern Plains than on those of the northern, that cannot be avoided. These are the Plains tribes we know best and with whom we have worked longest. If all the grants in aid we could have used had been available to us, the book would be more nearly complete.

We hope the old stories will blend with the new to bring you some pleasure, feeling, and understanding of Plains Indian oral literature.

INTRODUCTION

The Peoples of the Plains

To many Americans and to most Europeans, aside from anthropologists, the Plains Indians are the "typical Indians." They lived and hunted from Canada to the Sonoran desert in Mexico, and from the Mississippi River to the eastern slopes of the Rocky Mountains. And so, in a sense, they are "typical," for the people of the Great Plains come from many backgrounds and speak diverse languages. Non-Indian powwow clubs in Germany and France and the eastern United States, who diligently research and make their own costumes, modeled from those of the Plains Indians, often give little thought to the many roots of these clothes.

It would be safe to say that what is called the "classic" Plains culture began to develop about (A.D. 1700 with the coming of the horse, reached its full flower in the late 1700s, began to wilt in the first of the 1800s, and with the final great white invasion of the Plains.

The horse was responsible for the development of the "classic" Plains culture. The horse made the people mobile. They could hunt and kill more buffalo, follow the buffalo herds, and move across the vast open expanses of land. They were free from wandering along the river banks and moving in limited areas.

The first migrations to North America took place about 10,000 years ago. The people spread eastward and southward from Alaska following the waterways. Migrations and resettlement of people continued for

1

thousands of years. Between A.D. 500 and A.D. 1200 considerable migration took place. As today, people have always shoved each other around and had to make room for newcomers. Exactly when and where the Plains people came from is not completely clear as yet. But by 1700 we do know that many groups had moved to or near the margins of the Great Plains.

The Algonkin-speaking Cheyenne and Arapaho came to the Plains from the east, and their mythology reflects that fact. One of their myths concerns a water monster who still, they say, lives in the Mississippi River. An offering of tobacco must be made to him whenever the river is crossed. In 1939, at the Pan-Pacific exposition, the Cheyenne and Arapaho demonstrators of crafts pitched cigarettes into San Francisco Bay. Many Cheyenne and Arapahos, just to be on the safe side, still offer tobacco when they cross any large body of water. This is also true of their Canadian cousins, the Plains Cree, who formerly lived in Manitoba.

From the northwest to the southern Plains came the Kiowa, and they tell a myth that centers around "Devil's Tower," a monolith in Wyoming.

The Comanche also came from the northwest to the southern Plains, leaving their Shoshoni-speaking relatives, the Utes, Crow, and Hidatsa.

The Blackfoot, Gros Ventre, and Nez Percé stayed on and along the eastern slopes of the Rocky Mountains.

The Apache, Lipans, Mescaleros, and Tejanos, are usually considered as belonging to the southwest, but they had their day on the Plains, too, and in 1956 one old Apache man could still tell of a buffalo hunt on horseback in the short grass country. "It seem to me like a dreamed," he said in relating his story.

The Siouan groups, Oglala, Teton, Brulé, Miniconjou, Yankton, Santee, Assiniboine, to name a few in the northern plains. fanned out from the Great Lakes, while their southern cousins, the Osage, Omaha, Quapaw, Ponca, Oto, and Iowa came from the area drained by the Mississippi River. The Caddoan-speaking Wichita, Pawnee, and Arikara came from still further south.

All these peoples spoke different languages or dialects of languages. The astonishing thing is that after the arrival of the horse their material culture, their religion, and their whole life-style were almost homogeneous.

Before the horse, the Plains people lived relatively restricted lives

on or near the margins of the Plains. They often hunted out on the
Plains, but they could not go very far and they were limited as to how
much game they could kill because they had to carry the meat home in
their bags or load it on dog drags or backpacks.

Many of them inhabited semisubterranean earth lodges or structures
covered with mats or bark or mud. Summer and winter they went buffalo hunting, driving the game over the bluffs and killing and skinning
them where they fell at the foot of the cliff face. Otherwise, the people
gathered wild fruits and eatable grasses, raised crops, usually tended
by the women, of corn, beans, and squashes, while some women and a
few men planted and harvested tobacco, to be smoked as incense in ceremonies. The men hunted smaller game: deer, antelope, prairie dogs,
and gophers, among others. Wild turkeys and rabbits were often taken
in nets, especially by the northwestern Plains tribes, and wild doves
and prairie chickens, like ducks and geese, were hunted with bows and
arrows throughout the area. Terrapins were a good source of food, as
were soft-shelled water turtles, but in many tribes fish of any kind was
taboo as food.

The women of the eastern groups did some weaving of sashes and
belts, and made mats and bags by a twining technique, but most clothing was made from skins. Moccasins were of many styles, some of
them with rawhide soles, and in the southwestern part of the area
there are indications that sandals were sometimes worn.

The women also made pottery, chiefly undecorated utility wares, and
sherds have been found along the streams in all parts of the Plains
that have been excavated by archaeologists. The rivers were the roads
for Indians all over North America, and the Plains people were no
exception. They made round "bull boats" from buffalo hides stretched
on willow or dogwood frames to use when they crossed streams, but
they were not watermen like the Indians of the northwest coast region.

Plains Indians are generally thought of as horseback Indians chasing after buffalo or attacking white settlements, but in the beginning,
in their more settled existence, the dog was their only domesticated
animal. We have records of drag dogs, pack dogs, and hunting dogs;
they figured in myths and legends, and the Cheyenne and Arapaho ate
them ceremonially at the Sun Dance. There is no way of knowing
whether these dogs for feasting were specially bred or not; probably
not.

Dog breeding, also the work of women, was purposefully selective

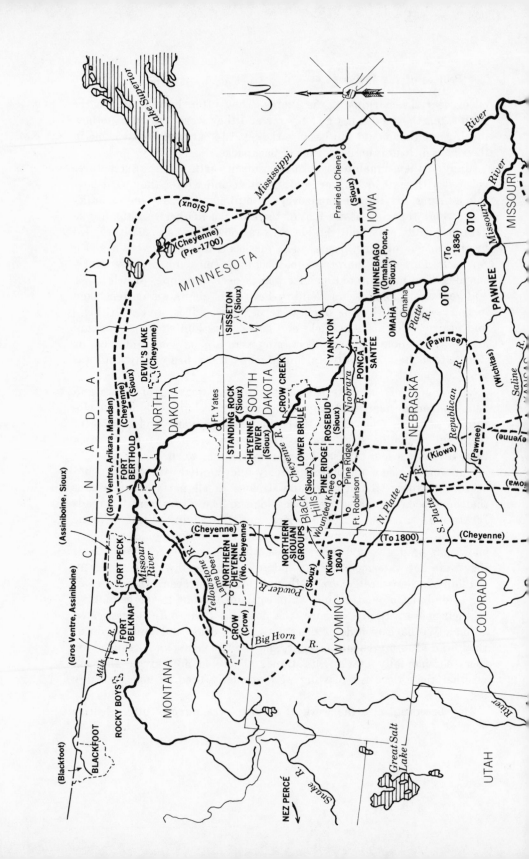

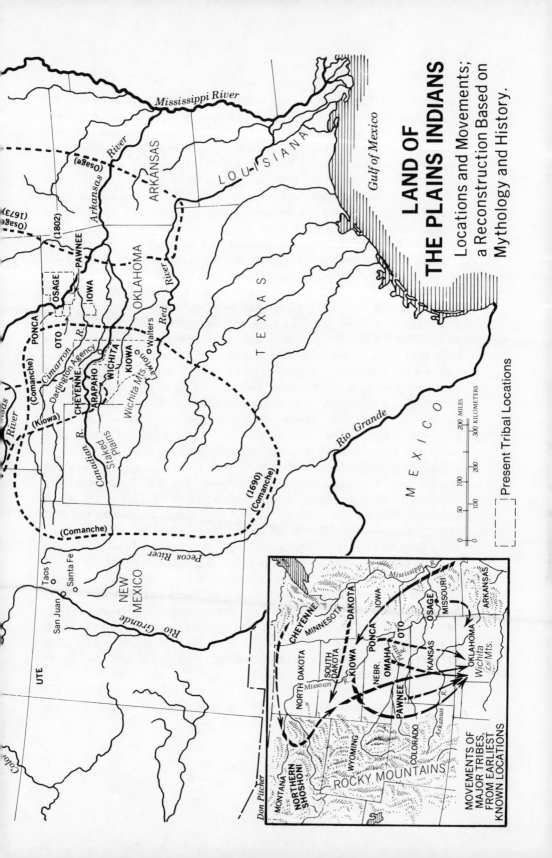

LAND OF THE PLAINS INDIANS

Locations and Movements; a Reconstruction Based on Mythology and History.

Mississippi River

Gulf of Mexico

LOUISIANA

ARKANSAS

(Osage)

Arkansas River

River

(Osage)(1673)

(1802)

PAWNEE

OKLAHOMA

IOWA

OSAGE

PONCA

OTO

Red River

Darlington Agency

Cimarron R.

CHEYENNE

ARAPAHO

WICHITA

KIOWA

Walters

Lawton

Wichita Mts.

Canadian R.

Staked Plains

(Kiowa)

(Comanche)

River

River

(Comanche) (1690)

(Comanche)

Pecos River

Rio Grande

NEW MEXICO

Santa Fe

Taos

San Juan

UTE

Colo.

Don Pitcher

Rio Grande

T E X A S

M E X I C O

200 MILES

300 KILOMETERS

50 100 200

100 200

0

Present Tribal Locations

MOVEMENTS OF MAJOR TRIBES, FROM EARLIEST KNOWN LOCATIONS

ROCKY MOUNTAINS

MONTANA

NORTHERN SHOSHONI

WYOMING

COLORADO

NORTH DAKOTA

SOUTH DAKOTA

Missouri R.

NEBR.

KANSAS

OKLAHOMA

Wichita Mts.

Platte R.

Arkansas R.

MINNESOTA

IOWA

MISSOURI

ARKANSAS

Mississippi R.

CHEYENNE

DAKOTA

KIOWA

PONCA

OMAHA

OTO

OSAGE

PAWNEE

(as horse breeding by men was to be) so that the puppies would be strong and healthy. Bitch and sire dogs must not be too closely related, but they should be similar in size and structure. The dam was not bred until after her second heat, so that the puppies would be stronger and she would be better able to feed them. During the first two heats the dam was isolated by being kept in the tipi or on a leash, close to her owner. At other times, all dogs were kept outside the tipis and had the run of the camp. There are many accounts of white men who came to Indian camps to be met by a swarm of dogs, followed closely by a swarm of women ordering their animals back to camp.

These animals were in no sense pets; the Plains Indians would have thought the very idea ridiculous. These were working dogs, always.

When the pups had been thrown, they were carefully selected. Indian women said, as professional breeders today do, that on the third day of a pup's life you could tell what the adult conformation and strength would be, and probably predict the adult disposition. All pups that did not pass the test were destroyed at once.

Since the dogs were sometimes used to pull drag loads on travois, it was not uncommon to dock their tails, for the sake of cleanliness. The ears were not trimmed, since there was no particular reason, esthetic or otherwise, to do so. Household goods, clothing, tipi covers, food, children, and puppies were dragged by dogs. A young strong dog could pull approximately one hundred fifty pounds.

Training the dogs began when they were about six months. Dogs had names, and were taught to come when called. The first light loads were attached to rawhide shoulder harnesses at about this time; usually a dog being trained was given only about ten pounds to pull for the first two or three months. More weight was added gradually until the maximum load was reached. Dogs were taught not to steal food from loads of game and not to fight when in harness, as Eskimo dogs still are.

We do not know how many strains of *Canis familiaris* originally came into the Americas. Several can be distinguished. Two types have been found in bundle burials at Mesa Verde: a small, curly-haired dog, rather like a spaniel, whose hair was probably used in weaving and braiding, and a larger, close-haired type that resembled the Plains drag or pack dog. The ideal pack or drag resembled a well-bred boxer in color, coat, and conformation.

What was it like, this country of sun and storms into which the Plains Indians emerged with their newly discovered horses? Overall,

the true Plains were once an ocean bottom, and they retain the rolling
forms of the waves which once passed over them. Some parts of the
Plains are flatter than others, but to think of Plains country in terms
of a tabletop is a mistake. Not only is there rolling land but there are
hills and canyons and "breaks" cut through the earth; mountains
border the Plains to the west and the Mississippi River to the east. The
true Plains stretch from eastern Alberta, Saskatchewan, and western
Manitoba in Canada to the Sonoran desert in Mexico. Wonderful
grasses covered this land, and bound its comparatively shallow soil in
mats that later iron plows had trouble penetrating. Bluestem, so tall it
was belly high on a horse, an almost endless variety of gramas, John-
son, and buffalo grass—all these grew on the Plains. Once they fed
buffalo and horses; now they feed cattle and sheep.

The relatively settled, rather stodgy life of the Indians that lived on
the fringes of the Plains was changed, almost magically, amost overnight, by the coming of horses. The people burst from the ground into
the sunlight. They became roamers, actually almost true nomads, for
they bred their horses and took the herds with them when they traveled.

Horses came to North America with the Spaniards, in 1540, but
Coronado's men had only enough horses for themselves. It was not
until 1598, when the colonizer Don Juan de Oñate brought brood
mares and jennets to the fork of the Rio Grande and the Chama
Rivers, that horse breeding became possible.

Some of Oñate's animals escaped from their pastures; some were
bartered for when the Indians saw their usefulness, and still others
were stolen outright. From San Juan Pueblo horses spread northward to the Canadian groups of Indians; eastward onto the Plains
between the Rockies and the Mississippi. With them went Spanish
ideas of horse trappings and breeding, and a complete change in
Indian cultures.

Life changed in many ways with the coming of the horse. Not only
did the people become mobile but pottery was discarded and weaving
almost forgotten; all but the simplest basketry was set aside. For
now, on horseback, with shorter, more powerful bows, the men were
able to bring in an abundant supply of buffalo, and everything a
household needed could be made from the dried or dressed hides.

Simple, cone-shaped shelters supported by poles and covered with
bark or hides, once used by hunting parties, became the towering deco-

rated tipis, for now it was possible to go into the mountains and bring back tall pine and cedar poles. Tipis and clothing and all manner of possessions were painted, for now it was possible to travel from a bed of clay of one color to that of another. Color preferences were shown; Cheyennes liked blue, Arapahos green, and Sioux preferred red.

In the south, the Kiowas and Comanches used little color but yellow, and much twisted fringe, to decorate their clothing; in the north, broad bands of earth- and vegetable-dyed porcupine quills were preferred. Everywhere, tipis were painted.

The social, religious, and economic structure of the Plains Indians also reflected the changes that occurred in the life of the people with the coming of the horse. New elements blended with older ones to form the cultures we know today.

Some tribes had bands, usually of unrelated members, and clans, of related members, usually matrilineal, but a few, like the Kiowa, were composed of only the bands. Marriage could be within the band, but not within the clan. It was usual to give a child a name that referred to its father's clan to strengthen the father's position. If the mother belonged to the wolf clan and the father to the eagle clan, for instance, their child might be named Flying Wolf.

Outside the family, band membership was important but could be changed. A man who disagreed with the band leaders might move to another band with his family, or, in some instances, simply establish a family camp. Such people were referred to by the Kiowa as "lonely band families."

The bands had both war and peace chiefs, who were represented in dealing with outsiders by interpreters, or "talking chiefs." Any man who had enough courage and faith in himself could recruit a war party if he wished, and if he were known to be successful in war could muster a large one. War parties were often away from camp for months, or they might make short forays against enemy tribes.

A peace chief was an older man, respected for his counseling. The office of the peace chief was not precisely hereditary, "It just got handed down in some families," as one Indian friend, himself, from a family of status, told us. The peace chiefs met annually, usually at the Sun Dance, and decided such matters as relations with other tribes or with non-Indians; where each band should hunt in the fall; what punishment should be doled out for adultery or other offenses, and the like.

But the real social control rested with the men's societies. Some, like those of the Arapaho, were rigidly age-graded; others, as with the Kiowa, were less tightly structured. Each society in its turn served as camp police, as game wardens on buffalo hunts, and many times the members of a society made up an entire war party. Members regarded each other as brothers, and used sibling terms in speaking.

Each society also had a "sister"; a young woman who danced with the members, and in some cases went on raids. Such women were highly regarded; they came from good families, and they had to be virgins. When a "sister" married, all members of her society had to agree in advance that the man who had asked for her was worthy of her. She could not marry into her own society.

Infant mortality was high, largely because of lack of knowledge of postnatal care. There were recognized midwives, some of whom were greatly skilled and who kept records of the children they delivered; one proudly showed an account book in which she had drawn the heads of eighty-six children she had delivered. Two faces were blank, to show that those children had died at birth.

Because of losses in warfare, there were more women than men in the Plains tribes. The surplus population was solved by plural marriages, but there was a general understanding that a man would not marry more women than he could provide for. Often the wives were sisters or cousins, because it was felt that there would be less friction in the home if the wives were related. If a man died, his brothers were expected to marry his wives. Often, said one Cheyenne woman, it was easier for children to know who was their father than their mother, since all women in a family shared equally in the care of all children.

Plains Indian religion was, generally speaking, pantheistic. There was a clear concept of an Above Person, who directed all activities on earth. Sometimes the Above Person was the Creator, sometimes he delegated this task to another supernatural. Everything and anything could have a spirit or be a spirit. Storms, landmarks, stars, and animals all were spirits and could become spiritual guardians.

A man acquired a spiritual guardian by going on a vision quest soon after puberty. He went alone and naked to a remote spot, taking with him only his pipe and his tobacco pouch. There he fasted and thirsted for four days, praying for mercy and blessing at least four times each day. Usually he received a manifestation of some sort: a lizard, a bird, an animal, or a strange cloud formation, perhaps. When his vision appeared, he was free to go home. Some men got their visions immediately, while others might have to make the quest several times. If a man still had not had a vision at the end of his fourth quest, he was pitied but not despised, but it was unusual for him to try again.

Before emerging on the Plains, tribes and individuals possessed ''bundles'' that contained personal, societal, or tribal tokens of spiritual power. After horses became part of Indian life, during the 1700s and 1800s, bands developed from villages and began to scatter over a wide area. There was a need for an annual general religious ceremony, and the Sun Dance came into being.

The Sun Dance is a renewal ceremony and a ceremony of thanksgiving. The men dancers fast, pray, dance, and smoke the sacred Indian tobacco for four days. In the 1800s and sometimes even today the dancers offered a piece of their flesh to the Creator.

The horse brought still more changes. Increased trade with other areas developed. There were recognized ''peace places'' for trading; fighting was banned for four days while goods were exchanged. War also became more prevalent, not just petty set-tos over who shot which deer first, but real war with organized soldier societies. Battle scenes and war fetishes were painted on tipis and shields. War parties went out and returned with captives, who were either adopted or enslaved, according to their age. And the white traders came, bringing such desirable items as cloth and beads and ribbons and whiskey and knives and bullets and guns.

And then it was gone, as suddenly as it began. Remnants survive today and are very precious. But the true, rip-roaring, snorting, waving, singing Plains Indian culture ended in the 1800s, when the white men hired by the railroads killed off the buffalo, almost to the last individual.

The Plains culture is the only Indian culture in North America of which we have a complete written history, for it could not have existed without the white man's horses and trade goods. The written records are various: missionaries' and soldiers' diaries, the trade goods lists of businessmen, and, at the end, newspaper accounts. Early-day anthropologists discovered that the Plains people were in general more outgoing and receptive to strangers than Indians in other parts of the country, and there probably was not one of the ''greats'' of anthropology —Alfred Kroeber, Robert H. Lowie, James Dorsey, George B. Grinnell, Robert Redfield, James Mooney, Frederic H. Douglas, Leslie

Spier, Clark Wissler—who did not leave at least one study of the Plains tribes on record. Alice Fletcher, Elsie Clews Parsons, Ruth Benedict, Gene Weltfish—women came later to study, but they came. And missionary and army wives sent letters home or jotted down daily notes. We ourselves have lived and worked and studied with Plains Indian tribes, and much of the material in this book has come to us firsthand.

It is impossible to categorize Plains Indians as "typical" of anything, and they themselves laugh at the idea. As LaDonna Harris, wife of former United States Senator Fred R. Harris, once said, "I'm a Comanche first, an Indian second, and then I'm an American." Tribal roots still are set deep in the soil that has been plowed, eroded, and in some places almost destroyed, and so it is still possible to study the Indians of the Plains. Here for your pleasure and for ours, are some of the tales they told and a few of the songs they sing.

PART 1

The Beginnings: The Great Myths

The Creation

PAWNEE

The Pawnees, who have been called "everybody's enemies," lived in the area of the present state of Nebraska, until they were removed by government pressure to Oklahoma in 1874. They are Caddoan-speaking and have many culture traits that are different from the more western Plains tribes. It has been postulated that the Pawnees represent the most recent of several northeastern Aztec migrations. The assumption is based on their midsummer sacrifice of a young woman to the morning star.

The woman, preferably from another tribe, was given the best of everything for the months preceding the sacrifice. When the time came, she was beautifully dressed and painted, her hair brushed and combed like a black river flowing over her shoulders. Then she was bound to a triangular scaffold, raised well above the ground. While the people watched, one of the priests drew his bow, and pierced her heart with a single arrow.

Against strong government protests, the Pawnee Morning Star sacrifice continued into the 1800s. Then, the story goes, a young Pawnee man, who had fallen in love with the captive, dashed through the crowd of onlookers on horseback, slashed the hide ropes that bound the woman to the scaffold with his knife, and rode away with her. The priests watched in consternation, and everybody waited for the end of the world, but the world went on and the sacrifice was never repeated.

15

Here, then, is the Pawnee story of how the world began. It contains many Aztec and Maya elements, and explains why a woman was sacrificed to the Morning Star.

The story of the vaginal teeth is found everywhere in the New World, and there are Asiatic and European equivalents.

First in the world was the Power. He was everywhere and nowhere. He was thought and planning; he was man and woman. He had everything that was and that would be.

"I need helpers," the Power said to Himself. "There can never be a world unless I have others to help Me."

He stretched out the four fingers of his right hand, and they became four stars. He put the Morning Star in the East, with the Sun to help and advise him. He set the Evening Star in the West, with the Moon to guide her. And the South Star and the North Star He put in their places in the heavens, with other, smaller stars as their helpers, because they are not as powerful as the Morning and Evening stars.

"Now show yourselves," ordered the Power, and the stars and the Sun and the Moon shone out in their places.

The Power looked around, and decided His world needed more shape. So He put the Black Star in the Northeast and the Yellow Star in the Northwest. He put a White Star in the Southwest and a Red Star in the Southeast. He said to the four stars He had just created: "You shall be known as the lodge poles of the heavens. It is your job to hold up the sky, and you shall stand as long as the sky lasts. And when men are made, you shall show them how to make sacred bundles for worshipping Me. You shall teach them to build their houses in the domed shape of the sky, and to set four lodge poles at the points where the roof beams are placed. Everyone will know what you can do, because, although your feet touch the earth, your heads touch the sky."

Then the Power sent clouds, winds, lightnings, and thunders to be the other helpers of the Evening Star. She put them between her and her garden, so later they could protect her and her crops. Immediately the elements became priests, each holding a great gourd rattle in his right hand. Now the Power was ready to create the world.

He told the Evening Star to order her priests to sing and shake their rattles. As they did so, a great storm came up and rolled across the still formless world. As it passed Him, the Power dropped a clear quartz pebble into the clouds. When the storm was gone, all the world was water.

Now the Power sent out the four colored stars, Black and Yellow, White and Red, each carrying a war club made of cedar, the sacred wood. When the stars came to the places where they were to stand, each of them struck the water with his club, and the waters parted, and the earth appeared.

Again the Power told the Evening Star to order her priests to rattle and sing, and again they created a great storm. The thunders shook the earth, so that its surface was no longer flat; thus, hills and valleys, mountains and plains were formed. Life could come to the earth now.

First He created the underbrush and timber. After another great storm, he put life in the plants so they could grow. With two more storms, the Power put life in the waters, and they began to move and the water creatures to move about in them. Then He made seeds for gardens, and put life in them. He made the birds and the animals, and gave them life.

Morning Star called all the star gods and the Sun and the Moon into a council.

"We must make a plan to create people to live in the world," he said.

"Should there be more than one kind of people?" Evening Star asked.

"Life can only come to people when there are men and women. We must make one of each kind," suggested North Star.

"How shall we do it?" South Star asked.

"You stars must mate first yourselves," Moon decided, and the Sun agreed with her.

"But how shall we know which two should mate?" South Star inquired.

"I am a woman," the Moon replied, "so it must be that Evening Star, whose helper I am, is a woman also."

"Why must the stars mate?" North Star demanded of the Sun. "If Moon is a woman and you are a man, then why don't you mate with Moon?"

"We are too powerful now," Sun answered. "Our mating might burn up all the world we have worked so hard to create. Morning Star

and Evening Star will have to mate first, then we can mate. That is the
only way the new world will be safe."

"How shall I reach the Evening Star?" Morning Star inquired.

"You must follow my path around the world until you come to
her," the Sun told him.

"But I don't want a husband," Evening Star protested. "Oh, Great
Power, help me. Protect me."

"I will help you," the Power promised her. "But I can't stop the
Morning Star if he discovers the way to mating."

The Power prepared to protect Evening Star by placing four fierce
animals around the world: wolf in the Southeast, with the power of
clouds; wild cat in the Southwest, with the power of winds; mountain
lion in the Northwest, with the power of lightning, and bear in the
Northeast, with the power of thunder. They, and Evening Star's four
priests, were her protectors and guardians.

"How can we best protect her?" the White Star asked.

"A woman is made like an animal," the bear said. "To mate with a
man, she must open her body to him."

"How can she do that?" Black Star asked. "A man is made like an
animal, but he is not one; a woman is made like an animal, but she is
not one. Even a young doe will fight a buck before she will let him
touch her."

"The female must suffer before she can bear children," Yellow Star
said. "Isn't it fair that the man should suffer, too?"

"What is the worst pain for a man?" Red Star asked.

"A wound in war," said the mountain lion.

"A snake's bite," said the wild cat.

The guardians all agreed that a rattlesnake could cause more pain
than any other living creature, and they sent for the Rattlesnake
Chief.

"Yes," he said, "we can cause great pain. But each of us has only
two teeth that carry poison. If we give up both teeth, we shall be as
helpless as garter snakes ourselves."

"We will take only one tooth from each of your young men," said
South Star. And so it was agreed.

Now the Power came back, and took one poisoned tooth from each
rattlesnake, and set them in a ring, pointing inward, between Evening
Star's legs and tightly against her body, like jagged rocks at the slope
of a canyon. "Stay here," he told her, and sent for Morning Star.

When Morning Star came, and saw what waited for him, he was

amazed. "How can I mate with this woman?" he cried. "I can't get near her! Oh, my helper, the Sun, show me what to do!"

"Wait for me," said the Sun, and he dived over the western rim of the world, and hid behind a big mountain of black obsidian. He chipped off a piece, as sharp as a knife, and found a round piece like a hand hammer. He brought the two pieces back to Morning Star.

"Knock the teeth out with the hammer and pry the roots loose with the knife," the Sun commanded, and the Morning Star obeyed. At last Evening Star lay helpless, and he was able to mate with her.

After a time a daughter was born, and she was the first human being, as her mother had been the first star. She stood on a cloud, and a whirlwind carried her down to the earth. Next, Moon and Sun married, and their child was a son, whom the whirlwind also carried to the earth.

Now the gods had to make a plan for humanity. They had to hold two councils before they could decide what to do. At last they called on the Power to help them. He directed Evening Star to bring out her priests, and they made rain fall on the two children. Then the children understood what the Power wanted them to do, and they mated as their parents had, and a grandchild was born. The Power instructed Evening Star to make more storms, and after each one the people understood better what they had to do.

The woman was taught about the earth, about planting and gardening, about how to make an earth lodge, taking its shape from the dome of the sky, about how to speak, and about the earth.

The man was dressed like a warrior and was taught how to travel over the earth and how to hunt and make war.

Many times after that Morning Star and Evening Star and their helpers returned to earth, and each time they came they taught the people more of the things men and women need to know.

Even today in the early spring the Pawnees recite their creation myth, in order to bring new life to the earth. Long ago they sacrificed a young woman captive to the Morning Star to repay him for his struggle in the creation.

Blanche Matlock, Pawnee.
A more detailed account of this story is in The Lost Universe *by Gene Weltfish, Basic Books, New York, 1965.*

The People of the Middle Waters and How They Came to Be

OSAGE

The Siouan-speaking Osages originally lived on the eastern margin of the true Plains, and displayed some traits of the Woodland tribes. As non-Indian pressure in the Mississippi Valley increased, however, the Osages moved westward at a measurable one hundred miles every ten years, until they became more and more a Plains people.

Many, many writers have recorded the doings and being of the Osages: their great vaulted rectangular dwellings shaped like beaver lodges and covered with mats; the star mats in which each of the thirteen Osage clans wrapped its magical possessions; the massive height and strength of the men and the delicacy and beauty of the women; their almost self-indulgent mourning of the dead; the Osage dominance in warfare, and their political manipulation of the diplomacy of three European nations in North America.

These were people of the rivers. They lived on the second rise of land above the streams; they planted and cultivated their gardens on the flood plains. Freshwater shells and the down of waterbirds were used in many of their ceremonies. No description of Osage watercraft other than the ubiquitous Plains "bull boats" has come down to us, but they probably used dug-out canoes at one time, for their physical and material resemblances to the people depicted on the shell carvings from the Spiro mound in southeastern Oklahoma are very strong.

Some of the Spiro carvings show people in boats, rowing with broad flat paddles. However, the Osage had probably abandoned the use of such craft—if, indeed they ever used them—long before recorded history began.

It is not surprising, therefore, to find that the myth of the origin of the Osage began on a river bank, possibly the Arkansas River or the Osage River, since both flowed through their territory.

It was spring, and the trees were fresh and their branches tender. The village chief of the beavers said to his people, "Let us begin now, and build a long row of lodges across the river, so that we will have warm homes when the winter comes." So all the men beavers set to gnawing down trees and building while the women went into the woods to gather fresh roots and berries to dry for winter food. They took their carrying baskets with them, and they packed their babies on their backs in flat wooden cradles, padded with thistle and swans' down and laced with strips of woven buffalo hair.

The village chief had a daughter who was very beautiful. She was not married yet, and usually her father watched over her closely. Many young men wanted to marry the chief's daughter, but those she liked her father disapproved of, and those he chose for her she found too old or too ugly. There was always something wrong with those men.

First came the wolf. "Give me your daughter," he demanded. "I am fierce and strong, and I can protect her."

"That would be good," the beaver girl said, "I always wanted to be protected."

"Give me your daughter," the wolf repeated, "or I will call for my brothers and make war on you. How can you, an old man like you, protect her if I decide to take her?"

"This way," said the beaver chief, and he took his daughter by the hand and they dived deep under the river and came up in their own house. The wolf ran up and down the bank and they could hear him howling as he went back and forth.

"Do you really want a husband like that, who acts like a bad child?" the beaver chief asked his daughter, and she hung her head and dropped her eyes, and whispered "No." All the same, she thought the wolf must be very strong, or he couldn't keep on howling that way.

Next came the wildcat. He purred and waved his tail in a soft curve, and he said to the beaver chief, "Let me marry your daughter."

"I don't know about that," said the beaver chief. "I think I ought to ask her how she feels." He liked the wildcat because he thought he had good manners.

When the daughter came, and saw the wildcat, and her father told her that he wanted to marry her, she thought it over, and then said, "How far can you swim?"

"Swim!" exclaimed the wildcat. "I never swim. I don't go near the water unless I'm thirsty."

"Then how can you cut down trees and build me a house in the river?" asked the girl. "See—all our young men are doing that."

"I don't build a house in the water," answered the wildcat. "I live in a cave in the Ozark Mountains."

"Live there alone, then," said the beaver girl. "I'm used to living in the water." And she dived down and down and came up in the house beside her mother.

The next suitor was the bear. He and the father smoked together, and talked about the old days when they were young men for a long time. Finally, the beaver chief sent for his daughter, and said, "I think this one would make you a good husband. He sits up the way we do, and he eats nuts and berries, and I know he isn't afraid of the water, because sometimes he goes fishing."

But the daughter looked at the bear, and said, "Father, I don't want to be rude, but he's as old as you are, and he isn't as handsome. Besides, what good is a husband that sleeps half the year? No, Father, I need a young, strong man."

And the bear laughed and shook his head and said, "My friend, there's no point in marrying a woman who's as stubborn as that. Good-bye." With that, he went away.

The beaver chief looked at his daughter and shook his head. "What am I going to do with you? You're a grown woman and ought to be married and raising a family. Think about it. You can't turn down everyone who comes around.

He shook his head again and frowned, and the daughter said, "All right, Father. I'll try to find someone who will suit us both."

One day during the spring building time the chief's daughter wandered away from the other women who were digging wild turnips. She got bored listening to them talk about their husbands and their children, and brag about how deep they could dive to get through the underwater doors of their lodges. Besides, she had a mat-bag of wild turnips, and her mother was gathering more with the other women.

So she walked along the river bank, picking up pebbles and mussel shells. She played with them and threw them away like a child, although she was at least fifteen years old.

Presently she saw a snail shell lying on the river bank, round and curled, striped brown and white. It was much more beautiful than the plain white mussel shells she had been playing with, even those with mother-of-pearl inside them, and it was larger than any snail shell she had ever seen.

"How pretty that is!" the beaver chief's daughter said, and she dropped the mussel shells she had been carrying and reached out her hand to the snail.

The snail uncurled from his shell and took her hand, and then he stood up before her, proud and handsome, strong and straight.

"Who are you?" asked the beaver girl.

"I am your husband," he answered.

"I don't know whether my father will give me permission to marry you," she said, turning her eyes away. "He has said no to some of the others."

"Let's go and ask him," suggested the snail.

So they walked slowly back, side by side, on the bank of the river, until they came to the great dam of lodges across the stream which was the beaver village.

"Father," said the chief's daughter, leading the snail into her father's lodge, "this is the man who has chosen me and whom I have chosen."

The chief thought a while. Then he asked, "Are you sure? Can he protect you?"

"Yes, Father, I am sure," she replied.

"Then you may marry him, for he is one of the water people," said the father, and he took the young man by the hand. "Stay here with us," said the beaver chief, "and you shall marry my daughter properly."

Then the chief sent for his four wives, and they came and dressed the girl for her marriage. They tattooed a spider on the back of each of her hands, to show that she was a woman and a chief's daughter. They painted her cheeks with red, as a sign that she was grown. And they put seven skirts on her, each tied with a separate braided sash, and seven blousês, each trimmed with mussel-shell buttons. They laid down seven mats for her to sit on, and six more for the snail-bride-groom, to represent the thirteen directions of the thirteen chief stars and the thirteen Osage clans that were to come.

Then the beaver chief blessed the young people, and the girl's mother placed a bowl of sweet meat and corn before them. She gave them each a wooden spoon, and they ate their first meal together. Then the beaver chief built them a house to live in, and so they were married. And in good time the beaver girl had a son, and then a daughter, and those two, who could be neither snails nor beavers became the first human beings to live on the land, and the first of all the Osages. People had come into the world, but they still built houses that look like the beavers'.

Teller wished to remain anonymous.

How the Earth and Men Were Made

ARAPAHO

The Arapaho were probably one of the first Algonkin-speaking people who moved westward out onto the Plains. Their oral history says that they came from the east, although from the country west of the Great River.

Apparently the Arapaho were never earth-lodge people, but always lived in cone-shaped, brush-, or hide-covered structures above ground. They were always primarily hunters. They have kept no tradition of pottery making or of basketry; as far as they themselves know, they have always used containers and carrying vessels of hide.

Three main divisions of the Arapaho are now generally recognized: the Gros Ventres of the prairie, or Big Belly people; the Southern Arapaho of Oklahoma, and the Northern Arapaho of Wyoming. The language of the Northern and Southern Arapaho has remained mutually intelligible.

Ties between the Northern and Southern Arapaho remain close because they share sacred ceremonial objects: the Flat Pipe, the Sacred Wheel, one ear of corn, the stone turtle figure, and the sacred paints.

The Sun Dance was known to the Arapaho as the Offering Lodge, in a considerably older form. The adaptation of the sun into its ceremony was relatively easy, since the Arapaho had always considered the sun's rays life—and health-giving. The rays were equated with the Wheel, and with the willow hoops across which buckskin thongs are laced like a spider's web, which are used in one of the men's games.

25

*The Arapaho have been closely associated with the Cheyenne,
and while some words in their languages are interchangeable, they
relied in early days on the sign language, and later on English as their
principal means of communication.*

*There is no clear evidence as to when the Arapaho first got horses.
In prehorse times, as today, women were dog breeders, and Arapaho
dogs were highly esteemed for their endurance in carrying drag loads
or backpacks. Probably, horses did not reach the Arapahos until the
middle 1700s.*

*Their earth origin legend is similar to those of many eastern Wood-
land tribes. It could be told only by certain persons, and those who
wished to hear it told from beginning to end had to fast for four days
before the telling started. Like many myths, that of the Creation
might be told only in the winter, "when the snakes were asleep." If
the snakes heard the stories they would take them away from the
people.*

———————•————————

First there was nothing but water. Flat Pipe was floating on its
surface. He was alone and lonely, but because he was a Creator he
could do something about it.

Man-Above, who has no form and can never be seen, spoke to Flat
Pipe. "You call on helpers," Man-Above said. "Ask them to help you
make a world."

So Flat Pipe thought of the water people, because, after all, he was
floating on water. He thought first of ducks, because ducks are water
birds, and as he thought of them the ducks appeared, floating around
him in the darkness. He could hear and understand their talking to
each other.

"Brothers," said the mallard, "Why are we here and why have we
been made? What is it we are to do?"

"Dive to the bottom of the waters, and bring me whatever is beneath them," Flat Pipe told the ducks.

"How deep are the waters?" the mallard asked.

"I have no way of knowing," Flat Pipe said, "They may be very
deep or they may be very shallow."

"Let the smallest try first, then," the ducks decided together. And
they chose the little teal to dive under the waters.

The teal was gone a long time, and when he came up he was gasping and panting and very weak. ''These waters are too deep for me to reach the bottom,'' the teal said when he was able to speak.

Then the mallard tried, and he, too, came up without having reached the bottom of the waters.

''You ducks mean well,'' Flat Pipe said, ''but I think we need some larger water birds.'' Then he thought of the great wild geese, and they flew onto the water from the north.

''Why are we here? What are we to do?'' the geese asked.

''We want to find out what is under the waters, so we can make a world,'' answered Flat Pipe.

''Have our brothers, the ducks, tried?'' asked the geese.

''They have tried, but they cannot reach the bottom of the waters,'' Flat Pipe told them.

So in their turn the great geese dived, and in their turn they came up with nothing. Then Flat Pipe thought that perhaps even larger water birds would be better, and he called for the swans.

''Be careful,'' Man-Above warned him. ''You have created three kinds of water beings. You can only make one more.''

''I will be careful,'' Flat Pipe said, but when the swans, too, returned without anything he began to despair.

''Perhaps you should make something that can live in the water or on the land, and is not a bird,'' Man-Above observed.

Flat Pipe thought for a long time, while he and the birds were floating around on the water. ''Land,'' he said. ''What is land? Perhaps it is something on which beings walk, and there can be beings without wings.'' And then he thought of the turtle, and it came swimming to him.

''Dive to the bottom of the waters, and bring up whatever is beneath them,'' Flat Pipe instructed her.

''I will try,'' the turtle said, and she dived.

She was gone so long Flat Pipe and the birds almost gave up hope, but Man-Above knew better than they did.

''Wait and see,'' he said. ''If Flat Pipe has done right, the turtle will be back.''

And sure enough, after more waiting, they heard the turtle's legs splashing in the water as she swam to Flat Pipe and spit a small piece of earth onto him.

''Well done,'' Flat Pipe said, and all the birds cheered with him.

"Now we will make a world." And the earth that Flat Pipe held began to grow and spread, and the birds sat on it and the turtle walked around on it, and they were all happy.

Then Flat Pipe took more earth, and made a man and a woman and a buffalo, so that they should all be together for the rest of time. He made other animals, too: deer and antelope and rabbits—everything that walks and runs. He made the war birds and the sacred birds, first the eagles and hawks, then the flycatchers, and then the songbirds.

"That is a lot of creatures," Flat Pipe said.

"Too many," Man-Above warned him. "Look, they are filling up all the space around you."

So Flat Pipe divided the land, and made an ocean; but not one as big as the first ocean on which he had floated. He made some new people, with light-colored skins and put them on the other side of the second ocean. "Stay there," Flat Pipe ordered. "Do not bother my people on the buffalo path."

But the light-colored people did not obey him, as we all know.

Lillian Toahty, Arapaho

How Men Were Made

CROW

The Crow Indians of the northern Plains were one of the many Siouan Groups. They were never a large tribe, but they were noted fighters and hunters among peoples who made their livings fighting and hunting. Crow men were among the tallest on the Plains, and they deliberately exaggerated their height by towering hair-dos, achieved by stiffening the hair with clay and pulling it up and back from the forehead. Crow men placed great value on hair, and also wore theirs long and flowing over their backs with many ornaments. When a man did not think his own hair was sufficiently abundant, he sometimes cut his wives' or gathered the hair that was cut off by people who were in mourning over the death of a relative, and plastered it to the ends of his locks with resin. Of course, this was a deliberate challenge to tribes with whom the Crows were at war to come and take the scalp-lock— if they could.

The Crows' own name for themselves is Absarkoe, which actually refers to the sparrow hawk, not the crow. Like many other tribal names it has been mistranslated so that the true meaning is distorted. Nothing could be farther from the familiar cornfield crow than the high-flying, swift-diving sparrow hawk.

The Crows, like other Plains Siouans, have a long and involved Creation myth, which through being passed from one generation to another has broken down into many little stories that explain the how *and why in the world. The Creation myth is well known to the Crows, but each person recounts it a little differently. The story that follows is only a fragment of the original Creation myth. It was collected in the early 1950s and varies somewhat from the versions collected in the first half of the twentieth century. The variation may be due to the differences in the storytellers' education and personality and to changes in Crow culture generally. Usually, the Creator is Old Man Coyote, who is the Trickster-Hero, but in our version the Creator is called "That Old Man Who Did Everything."*

That Old Man Who Did Everything, he was wandering around. There was nothing but water everywhere. He wandered over the water looking and looking. Out of nowhere he heard voices.

"I guess we are the only ones."

"I'm sure we are the only ones."

That Old Man Who Did Everything looked around until he saw four ducks. Two of them were blue-eyed ducks and two of them were little red-eyed ducks. The little ducks had been doing the talking. That Old Man Who Did Everything walked over to where the ducks had gathered.

"No you are not the only ones. I'm here," said That Old Man Who Did Everything. "Do you really truly believe that we are the only ones?" he asked.

The first big duck said, "No. Something in our hearts believes that there are other things."

"Yes. Go on and tell me. What do your hearts believe?" said That Old Man Who Did Everything.

"Well, we believe that maybe there is something way down in the water."

"Yes, yes, that is what I want to hear," said That Old Man Who Did Everything. "You can dive. Why don't you dive down and see what you can find?"

So the first duck dived down and down. He was gone a long, long time. "I'm afraid that my brother was drowned," said the other big duck.

"No, do not be afraid of that," said the first red-eyed duck.

"No, do not worry about that," said the second red-eyed duck. "He has not been gone long enough to have reached the point of being tired.''

So the ducks and That Old Man Who Did Everything sat and waited. After a time the first duck came to the surface. He was panting so hard for air they had to wait some more until he caught his breath.

''Well, younger brother, did you get anything?'' asked That Old Man Who Did Everything.

The first duck shook his head. ''No. I went down and I went down but I did not find anything.''

''I'll go down and see what I can find,'' said the second big duck. That Old Man Who Did Everything agreed and the second duck dived down deeply into the water.

Again they waited and waited and waited. ''I guess that my brother has died,'' said the remaining big duck. ''He has been gone so long.''

''No. Your brother has not died,'' said the first red-eyed duck. ''He has not been gone long enough to reach the bottom.'' They waited and waited and at long last the second duck appeared on the surface.

''Did you find anything?'' That Old Man Who Did Everything yelled.

''No,'' replied the second duck. ''I went down and down and down but I got nothing. I did see something down there but I could not reach it. I was too tired.''

''These big ducks cannot go down far enough to find the bottom. Let me go down,'' pleaded the first little red-eyed duck.

That Old Man Who Did Everything thought for a while. He looked at the red-eyed duck and thought some more. At last he agreed, but he cautioned, ''You are quite small so be very careful that you do not exceed your limit. I don't want any of you to die.''

The first red-eyed duck agreed. He dived down and down and down. He too was gone a long while and the others waited and waited. At last the first red-eyed duck broke the water upwards and came to the surface.

''Did you get anything?'' That Old Man Who Did Everything yelled.

''Yes!'' gasped the little red-eyed duck. ''I went down and down and down and something struck me. I looked where I felt it hit me and I took this.'' He handed That Old Man Who Did Everything a piece of a plant.

That Old Man Who Did Everything looked at it carefully. He turned it this way and that and you could see his face wrinkle with thought. At last he spoke. "Where this came from there must be earth. There is no doubt, my younger brothers, that what you felt in your hearts is true. There is something way down in the water." That Old Man Who Did Everything turned to the second red-eyed duck. "You go down this time. The other ducks are all too tired. If you feel something hard don't touch it. Keep going until you feel something soft. Don't look at it. Put some of it in your bill and bring it to me."

"I'll go. Right now," the second red-eyed duck answered excitedly.

Down and down and down and down he dived until he felt something hard with his feet. On and on and on and on he went until he felt something soft. He shut his eyes tightly and filled the hollow of his bill with it. It was sticky and he had a hard time pulling his feet loose. He swam upward as fast as he could with the soft stuff sticking to his feet. Upward and upward he went until he broke the water.

"Did you get something?" That Old Man Who Did Everything demanded.

The little red-eyed duck was so tired that all he could do was swim to That Old Man Who Did Everything and empty his bill into his hands and wipe his feet on his arms.

That Old Man Who Did Everything looked at the brown stuff in his hands and smiled. "It is mud!" he exclaimed. "It is wet earth. With this we can make our world. Are you ready?"

The two big ducks and the two little red-eyed ducks all yelled together, "We are ready."

That Old Man Who Did Everything and the ducks made the world. Then they divided the world into sections by placing water here and there. They made the sky, the plants, the trees, and the animals. They made the stars and the sun and the moon. After a long while That Old Man Who Did Everything decided that was not enough so he made the people.

He made the people out of clay as he had made everything else. He made three groups of men and women. He set them on the ground in front of him, while he made some clay arrows. He put the arrows in a row on the ground a long way away from him.

Then That Old Man Who Did Everything said to the clay people, "I do not know which group of you is the bravest. I want only brave people. I will test you to find out. Run. Run through the arrows, and the one that goes through them will be my people, and will learn many things!''

The first group started to run, but when they came to the row of arrows they were frightened and stopped in their tracks. They could not go on, and they fell to the ground.

''Get up,'' ordered That Old Man Who Did Everything. ''Go away. You cannot be my people.'' Then he told the second group to run through the arrows, but they were frightened, too, and turned back.

''Go like the others,'' That Old Man Who Did Everything said to them.

Nobody knows anymore who these two groups of people were. They were Indians, but what Indians has been forgotten.

Now That Old Man Who Did Everything told the third group to run through the arrows, and they did. If they were frightened they did not show it.

''You are very brave people,'' said That Old Man Who Did Everything. ''You will be my people, and I will give you helpers to teach you. Where you live shall be the center of the world.'' That is why the Crows lived in Montana and Wyoming, between the mountains and the plains, and beside the Yellowstone River, and why all the other tribes respected and feared them.

Told by a Crow friend.

Emergence Myth

KIOWA

Culturally, the Kiowa present an enigma to ethnographers. Their written history probably begins with a Spanish chronicle of 1732, which places them in Montana at the extreme head of the Missouri River. Apparently the Kiowa already had horses at that date, because there is mention of their cutting pine trees for lodge poles, and such tipi poles would have had to be dragged by horses.

In other ways, the Kiowa are distinctly southwestern, and probably the encounter on the Upper Missouri River was due to a dearth of lodge pole pines nearer home. Such forays away from home base were common practice among all the southern Plains tribes.

The Kiowa material culture lacks the elaboration of decoration found among the northern tribes. Porcupine quills, which were used for decoration by the northern tribes, were taboo to them, so the women made no quillwork. Although beads and metal were readily accessible through Mexican traders, the Kiowa, like the Comanche, preferred to decorate their clothes with earth paints or with very narrow bands of fine beadwork. The Kiowa women also were noted for their lavish use of fringing, finely cut and tightly twisted, on both men's and women's clothing. These traits are reminiscent of the Rio Grande Pueblos, where dance garments are still painted and never beaded, and where the long, sweeping swing of a properly tied "rain sash" or "bride's belt" is a pride and joy.

*Similarly, the Kiowa origin myth is in the southwestern manner.
Unlike the peoples of the northern Plains, the Kiowa do not tell of
earth diving, but of emergence from an underworld. Pueblos and
Navahos alike tell of people coming to the upper world through a
hollow reed; in the case of the Kiowa, it was a hollow log. In either
event, men and women were fully formed when they came into the
sunlight, and there is no account of a Creator's experimenting before
he perfected human beings. Like many other myths, this one has
become fragmented, and only a part of the whole can be told. It fea-
tures the Trickster-Hero, Saynday, in his heroic role.*

■ ▬▬▬ ◄ ■ ▬▬ ■

Saynday was coming along, but it was hard work, because everything was dark. He kept bumping into people, and everytime he did it,
he said, "Ouch!" Then the other person said, "Ouch!" too, but nobody knew who anybody else was. Saynday began to get tired of it.

"Come here around me, everybody," Saynday shouted at last.
"We've got to do something about this!"

In the darkness he could hear the rustling and the bumping as the
people clustered together. Just to make sure he didn't get knocked
down, Saynday put on his left hand. He felt something rough standing next to him, and he felt as far around it as he could. It was a tree
trunk.

Saynday felt up the tree trunk as far as he could, but he could find
no branches. Then he felt down it, to the ground, and there he found
an opening, big enough for a man to crawl through.

Saynday held out his right hand, because he was left-handed and
had kept hold of the tree trunk with that hand. He took hold of the
person next to him. "You take somebody else," he instructed.
"Everybody take hands and follow me."

Then Saynday crawled into the tree trunk, and began to climb. It
was narrow, so he could brace himself with one arm on each side of the
opening. The other people climbed behind him, but they could no
longer hold hands because they had to use two hands to climb with.
But they all went along steadily, following each other by the sound of
feet, and at last Saynday saw a tiny opening above his head. As he
went on climbing, the opening grew larger.

At last Saynday put his arms over the edge of the hole and heaved

himself out of the tree trunk. He was standing on the ground, and the
tree still rose above him. Other people were coming out of its trunk
now, and looking around them, and laughing and blinking.

"Well, Saynday," one old lady said. "Here we are. What shall we
do next?"

Saynday looked around. The tree stood on a river bank, and was
part of a grove of cottonwoods. On the other side of the river the prairies rolled away, covered with thick, short grass, and on the grass were
deer and antelope grazing.

"I'm hungry," said one little boy. "Let's get some food."

"That's a good idea," Saynday remarked. "Let's all make some
bows and arrows and go hunting."

But the only wood they could find at first was cottonwood, and it
snapped and splintered when they tried to break it evenly.

"This stuff's no good," Saynday said, and he threw it away.

"You'll be sorry for that sometime," said the cottonwood tree. "I
brought you here, and sometime you will need fire. I can give you the
best firewood there is."

"Well, right now I need something to cook over that fire," Saynday
answered. "Where shall we go for hard wood?"

"Try bois d'arc [boe dark] and dogwood," said the cottonwood
tree. "They're hard enough and straight enough for what you need
now."

So Saynday and the other men hunted up and down the river bank
until they found dogwood, but it took a longer time to find bois d'arc,
because that grew on the outer edge of the grove, almost on the open
prairie.

Then Saynday used his magic power to make stone knives and
points. They cut the branches they needed with the knives, and tied
the points on the sticks with buckbush branches. Then they twisted
grapevines to make bowstrings, and for the first time all the Kiowa
men went hunting.

With the skins of the deer and antelope, the women made clothing,
for up until then they had all been naked. It didn't matter underground, but on the top of the earth they couldn't help seeing each
other, and they didn't think that was very nice.

The men took the sinew from the animals, and twisted it into hard
cords and string, for bowstrings and arrow bindings. Then they could
bring in more and more game because the sinew was stronger than the
branches and vines.

The Kiowa lived on the edge of the prairies for a long time, until there were so many of them they decided to divide into two bands.

"Before we do that," said one of the old men, "let's go hunting together one more time."

So all the men gathered together the next morning, and soon they found a herd of antelope. They shot several, one of them a young doe with a full udder.

"I'll take that," said a friend of the man who had shot the doe. "My wife sure likes that tender meat."

"No," said the man who shot it. "I'm going to take it to my wife. She likes it, too."

"I want it," his friend insisted. Ever afterwards, a Kiowa has had to give his friend what was asked for, but the rule hadn't been made yet. Instead, they quarreled all afternoon.

Sayday came up while they were arguing and listened for a while. He was disgusted.

"Oh, shut up," Sayday said, finally. "You were going to split up into two bands anway. Now, let the man who shot the doe take it and go away to the north, and let anyone who wants to go with him. The others can go away to the south, and that will be that."

And so they did, turning their backs on each other and walking away without saying another word. The ones who went to the south called themselves the Real Kiowas, and they called the band that went north the Udder Band.

The two bands never met again, but the Kiowas are still looking for the Udder People. Sometimes they think they have found them. Once some Kiowa men heard Crow men talking, and thought that they were speaking the same language, but they were not, after all. Another time, some Kiowa went to a dance at Taos Pueblo, and they thought they recognized words the Taos people said, but that was a mistake, too. The two bands have never found each other again.

And that's the way it was, and that's the way it is, to this good day.

＊━━━━＊＊━━━━＊

Maude Campbell, Kiowa

Grandmother Spider and the Twin Boys

KIOWA

There is a pronounced dichotomy in Kiowa life. There is the Saynday cycle of stories, in which the main character is alternately Trickster and Hero; sometimes both. But there is also a ceremonial cycle, which can be told only by certain persons and at certain times. Saynday stories are told in the winter; the ceremonial cycle in summer.

In the same way, the Kiowa had two orders of men's societies: the usual Plains war societies, more or less age-graded, from the Rabbits, which boys joined when they were six or seven and from which they graduated at puberty to the Herders or other societies, such as the Gourd Dancers and others. All aspired to membership in the Bravest of the Brave—the ten war chiefs who made up the Crazy Dog Society.

Paralleling the soldier societies were the sacred societies, with secret rituals and passwords. They were known as various types of shield societies, and their members were feared by other Kiowas as magicians. Even the Buffalo Shields, whose chief concern was with healing, were held in awe because it was believed that much of their curing was accomplished by magic. Women had societies also, the names of at least two of which have come down to us: The Buffalo Women "were for dancing," while the Bear Women formed a counterpart of the shield societies and were feared in the same way.

Bears are still sacred beings to the Kiowas. The Kiowas do not say the true word for "bear" even today, but use a synonym. They will

*not eat bears, or look at them, or go near trees where bears have sharp-
ened their claws. In these taboos they resemble the tribes west of them,
especially the Navahos and other Athabascans.*

*The Kiowas have a story cycle, concerning Spider Grandmother, her
grandsons, the War Twins, and their adventures. It is hard to find
another such cycle among the Plains Indians. The closest comes from
the Pueblo and the Navaho, and again suggests more contact with the
southwest than is generally recognized.*

*The Kiowa sacred cycle concerns the tribal medicine bundles, the
Ten Grandmothers, and it cannot be told in its entirety. Probably no
Kiowa now alive has heard the complete cycle. Each Grandmother
bundle had two guardians, a man and a woman. It is said that originally they were brother and sister, but by the 1890s the guardians of
each bundle were only distantly related.*

*The guardians gathered, with their bundles, at the time of the
annual Sun Dance. Each bundle in turn was opened, and its part of
the myth was told. The Grandmothers were the guardians of the
Kiowa, and their chief function was to gather up all evil that might
befall the people—in a sense, they were spiritual vacuum cleaners.*

*The Grandmothers still exist, though their whereabouts are a closely
guarded secret. What follows is only a fragment of the great story,
told by one of the guardians who had become Christian, and who shall
be nameless.*

◆━━━━◆◆━━◆ ◗

After the Son of the Sun became two, they were called the War
Twins. They still lived with Grandmother Spider, and every day, after
they had helped her with the garden, she taught them more and more
of the things that men should know.

From their Grandmother the Twins learned to make bows and
arrows. They learned to dry buffalo sinew and braid boestrings. They
learned to make the arrows with the feathers bound with sinew and
spiraling around the arrow shafts. They learned to make spears, with
sharp quartz points. And they learned to make shields, but they did
not yet paint their shields, because they had not earned that right in
warfare. They were still just boys.

Now, one morning, a woman came to Grandmother Spider's tipi
crying bitterly.

"What is the matter?" Grandmother Spider asked her.

"A great bear came out of the east," the woman sobbed. "He seized my man, and there, in front of the tipi, he ate him."

"That is very bad," said Grandmother. "Bears are dangerous. They stand up like men and they can mate with human women. The bear children will kill and eat their mothers and their brothers and sisters. I will send my grandsons out to kill that bear."

But before the boys could start, another woman came crying that a bear from the north had killed her man, and soon after that other women came weeping because their men had been killed by bears from the south and the west.

"You are very young to start having your war adventures," Grandmother Spider said to the boys, "but you will have to go now. Maybe it is just one bear going around the camp like the sun—or maybe there are four bears. You are the Sons of the Sun, and nobody can kill the bears but you. Be careful. Stay together always. And when you have killed a bear, bring me part of it, so I can be sure."

So the boys set out, traveling to the east with their bows and their quivers of arrows on their backs, and their spears and their shields in their hands. For four days they traveled eastward, until they found a great bear standing on his hind legs, facing them. And the bear not only stood like a man but he fought like a man, using his teeth for knives, until the Twins stuck their spears right through him, one from each side, and he fell down dead. Then they cut off his ears, and took them home to Grandmother.

"Good," she said when she saw the trophies, and she took the ears and hung them over the smoke of the fire to dry. "But this is only one bear. You had better go out again and be sure there *is* only one."

The Twins traveled to the south, and to the west and to the north, and each time they found a bear and killed it. And each time they cut off the bears' ears to take home with them.

While they were having their adventures, Grandmother was busy at home. First she made eight cases of the finest white-tanned fawnskin. In each case she put a bear's ear. Then she made painted rawhide cases to hold the fawnskin bags. When the boys came home the last time, she told them:

"Now you can paint your shields, and when you have done that, give them to me. I will put them in cases like these trophies you have brought, so there shall be ten holy things to guard the people."

"What designs shall we paint on the shields?" the Twins asked.

"Bear and lightning designs, so the Kiowas will have great power in time to come," Grandmother instructed them.

Four days the Twins soaked sinew in water to make glue. Then they mixed the glue with earth colors. One brother painted a bolt of lightning on his shield and the other brother painted a bear on his. The painting took them four days and all four days they fasted. At the end of the time they took the shields to Grandmother Spider, who had been fasting, too. She put the shields in the cases she had made for them.

"Now let us all take sweat baths, and clean the bear power off our bodies," Grandmother said. She went into the sweat lodge first, and the Twins rolled hot stones in to her, and passed a bucket of water and a bunch of sage in, so she could rub herself clean. When Grandmother had rid herself of the bear smell, the Twins went in together, and she heated rocks and passed the water and sage to them.

"Let the people remember this," Grandmother Spider said. "Whenever they touch holy things, or even look at them, they must sweat and rub themselves with sage before they eat anything. And then they must eat very little, and drink only a little water until the next day." She made some broth, and they all drank that and a little warm water, and went to bed praying.

And this is what the Kiowas still do when they take part in a ceremony or are asking for a blessing.

Storyteller's name withheld by request.

The Ghost Owl

CHEYENNE

The Cheyenne probably came to the Plains after their cousins, the Arapaho, were established there. The early Cheyenne range, over a period of years, was from Minnesota to Montana. They were made up of two groups, the Tsistas and the Suhtai, whose languages were mutually intelligible. There are still two Cheyenne groups, one in Montana and the other in Oklahoma, but their members come from both the original groups.

The Cheyenne probably did not have horses until well into the 1700s, and remained earth lodge people for a few years afterwards.

The Cheyenne of both groups tend to be more reserved than the Arapaho, to have fewer contacts with strangers, and to, in the old phrase, keep themselves to themselves. We have been fortunate enough to have been adopted into a Cheyenne family ourselves, however, and have seen many ceremonies and heard many stories.

The Cheyenne do not fear bears as the Kiowas do, but they have a great respect for them, as the ancestors of all human beings. Once, during a night in Yellowstone Park, an old Cheyenne woman called out, "Come! Come quickly! The ancestors are eating the garbage!" Following the culture pattern of Yellowstone Park bears, the ancestors had indeed overturned the garbage cans, and were feasting.

Personal spirit guardians in animal form were also deeply respected by the Cheyenne. Not only was there a food taboo associated with the

*guardians, it was considered deeply improper to mention their names
in the presence of those they protected. An outsider might be warned,
"Don't say 'crow' to that man. It's sacred to him." How these taboos
were learned about has never been made quite clear. No one was supposed to tell who his spirit guardian was.*

*Terrapins also were sacred. Probably there had once been a terrapin
clan, although it has disappeared now. Male and female turtles were
distinguished by the coloring of their legs; a female's legs were yellow
and a male's red. A child's navel cord was encased in a buckskin cover
shaped like a turtle, made only by certain women. And only women of
certain families might make fry bread in the form of a turtle at ceremonial feasts.*

*The fear of owls, as ghosts returned to earth for many reasons—
revenge, to complete incomplete tasks, and to fulfill physical needs that
were not satisfied in life, to name a few—is so widespread in North
America that it cannot be pinpointed to any one group. All Algonkian
and Athabascan people know it, and fear of Tecolote, the ground owl,
is widespread in Mexico. The fear of the owl is a different thing from
fear of the bear; it is a complete physical dread of the night bird. The
story that follows probably dates from earth lodge days.*

<hr />

A little girl sat crying in her mother's lodge. She was angry because
her mother wouldn't let her do what she wanted to do. It was night
time, and her mother told her she couldn't go out of the lodge.
Finally, the mother got so exasperated that she picked the little girl
up and put her outside.

"Go on," the mother ordered. "The owls can have you if they want
you."

It happened that there was an owl just outside the lodge, sitting in a
tree, waiting for a mouse or a rabbit to come along. When he saw the
little girl, he swooped down and picked her up in his claws and flew
away with her. He carried her off to his lodge where his old grandfather lived.

"Here," the owl said, "This is something nice for you to have."

"Good," said the owl grandfather, and he clapped his wings
together for pleasure. "You can sleep in that corner," he told the
little girl, pointing with his lips to the women's place on the south side

of the lodge, ''and in the morning you can get busy and make yourself useful.''

When the little girl woke up the next morning, the owl grandfather sent her out to get wood for a fire. ''If you don't work, you can't eat,'' he said. ''I can't stand daylight, so you'll have to do the outside work, except at night.''

As the little girl went through the woods, picking up sticks and dry branches, a sparrow flew up to her. ''You're gathering that for yourself,'' said the sparrow. ''They're going to cook you and eat you.'' The child was frightened, and ran back to the owl's lodge, because it was the only place she knew to go.

''That isn't enough firewood,'' the grandfather said. ''Go on. Go out and get a big pile. Nobody can cook with those little old sticks.''

So the girl went out again, and this time a flycatcher flew up to her and warned her that she was going to be eaten. She ran back to the lodge and piled the wood on top of what she had already brought.

''That still isn't enough,'' scolded the old owl. ''How am I going to get any dinner from that little heap?''

A third time the girl went out, and this time a red-winged blackbird warned her, ''Don't do that. You're gathering it for yourself.'' And again she was frightened and ran back to the lodge.

''You'll never make a man a good wife,'' said the old owl, glaring at her. ''Why, you can't even gather enough firewood to cook a meal.''

Once again the girl set out to gather wood, and this time a red-tailed hawk flew up to her. ''This is the last time,'' he said. ''We have all tried to warn you. Now you must not go back.''

''What shall I do?'' the girl asked. ''Where can I go to be safe?''

''Get on my back,'' the hawk said. ''I will take you to a safe place on a high mountain, and I will tell you what to do when you get there.''

So the girl put her hands on the hawk's shoulders, and he carried her away and away, up to the top of a high mountain, and on the way he told her what to do when they got there. The hawk landed right in front of a big rock on the mountain top.

''Now do just what I told you,'' he ordered.

The girl said to the rock, ''My hawk grandfather, I have come to you for protection. My hawk father, I have come to you for protection. My hawk brother, I have come to you for protection. My hawk husband, I have come to you for protection.''

Then she heard a voice say, "You will be safe here." The rock rolled aside, and there was a big cave. At first the girl was afraid to go in because she saw only the old hawk grandfather sitting there. "Come on, I won't hurt you," he reassured her, and she went in. Behind her the rock rolled back in its place.

When the old owl realized that the girl had escaped, he was very angry. "Those hawks must have played this trick on me," he said, "but I'll get her back. They can't keep her forever."

He started out for the mountain. Four times on the way he stopped; each time he hooted four times, and when he hooted the earth shook. The girl heard him coming and was terrified. The fourth time the owl hooted he was right outside the door.

"Bring out my meat," he howled. "If you don't, I'll come in and get it."

"Open the door just enough for him to get his head in," the hawk grandfather directed the girl.

She opened the door, and the owl thrust his head in. Then she slammed the rock back in place, and cut his head off so it rolled around on the floor.

"Roll the head out of the lodge with a stick," said the hawk grandfather. "Don't touch it, or any part of the body. Make a pile of dry wood and I will come out and help you."

They did so, and when the pile was big enough, the hawk grandfather set it on fire, and threw the head and the body on top of the flames. The body split open and all kinds of beads and pretty things came rolling out. The girl wanted to pick them up, but the hawk grandfather made her throw everything back in the fire with sticks for tongs.

Then they went back in the lodge, and the girl stayed with the hawks until she was grown up. She did a woman's work, and she became very beautiful. But she still missed her own people, and finally she told the hawks so.

"Well, you are old enough to take care of yourself now," the hawk grandfather said. "But you must do just exactly what I tell you if you are to get back safely."

"I will," the girl promised.

Then the grandfather made her a red-painted robe, and had her make a boy's moccasins and leggings. The grandfather made her a thunder bow with lightning designs on it, and he fastened buffalo bulls' tails to the heels of her moccasins to wipe out her tracks. Last he

painted her face red, and tied the skin of a prairie owl on her forehead. She was dressed like one of the Backward-Talking Warriors, who
were the greatest warriors of the Cheyennes, not like a girl.

When she was ready to leave, the grandfather gave her a live mink.
"Keep this inside your robe," he instructed her. "Never let go of it.
Then when you start out, pass by the first four villages you come to.
On the evening of the fourth day you will come to your last great
danger. An old woman will come out of her lodge and call to you and
offer you food. Don't eat any of the first bowl; feed it to the mink. The
second time she will give you buffalo meat and you will be safe to eat
that. Be sure you keep the mink with you, but let it go when the old
lady threatens you."

It all happened just that way. On the fourth evening the girl came
to the old lady's lodge, and the woman came out and called to her,
"Come in, my grandson. You must be tired and hungry."

So the girl went into the lodge, and the woman fixed her a bowl of
brains cooked with mush, and gave her a horn spoon to eat it with. The
girl pretended to eat, but instead she fed the mush to the mink.

"My, you are hungry, grandson," said the old woman. This time she
gave her dried buffalo meat, and the girl ate it.

"Lie down and rest," said the old woman, and she took the bow
with lightning designs on it and hung it on the west side of the lodge.
Then she spread out some hides in the man's place on the west side of
the lodge and the girl lay down on them and pretended she went to
sleep. She even snored a little. "I'll stay up a while and keep the fire
going to warm you," said the old lady.

As soon as she thought the girl was asleep, the old woman sat down
by the fire and began to scratch her leg. She scratched until the leg
swelled up into a great club. Then the woman started for the girl to
beat her to death, but the girl let the mink out of her robe. The mink
ran across the floor and bit a big chunk out of the woman's leg.

"You've killed me!" she screamed, and fell down dead, while the
mink ran away.

The next day the girl went on again, and that night she came to her
own village. Everyone came running out to see who the handsome
young man was. They all asked her questions, but she was ashamed to
say she had been so naughty when she was little that her mother had
given her to the owls. She hung her head and would not speak.

"Who are you? What tribe are you? Where have you come from?"
all the people asked her.

At last she said, "I am the naughty girl whose mother threw her
away. I have had a hard time and come through many dangers, but
now I am back with my own people."

Then her mother came to her, weeping and crying to be forgiven.
And some young men came to her, and asked if they could wear the
same kind of clothes she had on. The girl thought a while and then she
said, "Yes. But because I am a woman dressed like a man, you must
always do some things backwards. If you are in battle, and someone
tells you, 'Go forward,' then you can go back." And that is how the
great soldier societies of the Cheyennes got started.

Mary Little Bear Inkanish, Cheyenne

PART 2

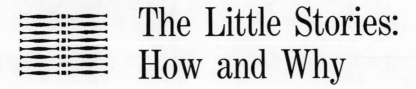 The Little Stories:
How and Why

Teaching the Children

KIOWA-APACHE

Almost every story a Plains Indian child heard taught him something. It was schooling in manners and behavior and ethics. It also taught that vigor and virtue would be rewarded, in some way, after the child grew up. The Kiowa-Apache story of the Dirty-Nosed Boy is an example. Versions of it are also told in other tribes.

The Kiowa-Apaches probably represent a late wave of migration into the Plains from the northwest. Their language is Athabascan, and related to the speech of the northern Athabascans proper, to that of the Navaho, and to those of the scattered Apache groups throughout the southwest. Still, their material culture is almost indistinguishable from that of their neighbors, the Kiowa or Comanche.

They had no Sun Dance but they had a separate place of their own in the Kiowa Sun Dance camp circle. They kept some of their old religion, including the masked dances of the Mountain Spirits which had originated, probably, in the southwest. Their myths and legends are closely related to those of the Kiowa.

So is the method of telling: around the fire, at night, in winter, with the grandfather beginning a story, and, at its conclusion, asking the next in the circle to "tie a tale on that." Not only the seasons and the sequences of years had their cycles but so did storytelling. As we already told you in the Arapaho story, "How the Earth Was Made," remember to tell a story at night in winter, "when the snakes are asleep," so they will not take the story away from you.

51

There was an old woman who was very poor. All her relatives were dead except her grandson, who was too young to hunt big game. They lived on rabbits and prairie dogs, and whatever fruit the old lady was able to gather.

That boy must have been part white! It seemed as if his nose was always running. People called him Drip Nose Boy because of it.

But Drip Nose Boy was good to his grandmother and did everything he could to help her and take care of her. As soon as he was old enough, he went to Mountain Man, who was the best bow maker in the village.

"Come in, Grandson," said Mountain Man, who was a cousin of Drip Nose Boy's grandmother. Sit down. Why did you come to me?"

"Thank you, Grandfather," answered Drip Nose Boy. He wiped his nose on his sleeve and sniffled a little. "Grandfather, I have come to ask you a big thing. I am almost afraid to say, it is that big."

"What is it, Grandson?"

"It's the biggest favor one man can ask another."

Grandfather almost smiled, because Drip Nose Boy was so little and thin from never quite having enough to eat that he could only be a child. But he stopped himself in time, and said, very soberly, "What is the favor you want to ask?"

Drip Nose Boy sniffled again and said, "I want to learn bow-making power."

Grandfather sat silently for a long time, looking at the little fire in the tipi floor. "What will you do with bow-making power if you have it?" he finally asked.

"I will make my own bow, and if it is good I can shoot deer and antelope for my grandmother to eat."

"And what else?"

"If it is very good, perhaps other people will want my bows. Then I can get her some cloth from the trading post to make new clothes and maybe a horse for her to ride on when we move camp."

"And what else again?"

"If my bows are *very* good, when I am older, perhaps I can shoot buffalo so she can always have enough to eat."

"What do you want for yourself?"

"Nothing," Drip Nose Boy replied.

Again Mountain Man was silent a long time. When he spoke he was very serious. "A long time ago, I went out to look for power. It came to me from a cedar tree on a mountain top. I smoked and prayed and cried and fasted for four days, until the cedar tree had pity on me. 'You can have power,' it said. 'You can use my strength to make bows. And if anyone ever comes to you for this power, you can give it to him, if he wants nothing for himself.' "

Mountain Man waited a moment. "You are the first who ever came to me wanting nothing for himself. You will be a fine young man. But you must do what I tell you. Go to the top of Mount Scott, where the oldest, strongest cedar trees in the Wichita Mountains grow, and make your vision quest beside one of them. Then come back to me."

"I will," Drip Nose Boy promised.

Mountain Man lent Drip Nose Boy a pipe, because he had none of his own, and Drip Nose Boy went away to the top of Mount Scott. There he found an old, twisted cedar tree, and sat down beside it. For four days he fasted and smoked and asked the tree for its help. At first he wondered why the tree, so bent and curved by the wind that never stopped blowing, should have bow power. Then he remembered that Apache bows were not like the ones used by other tribes, but had an in-curve in the middle, like the cedar tree.

On the fourth night of his vision quest, Drip Nose Boy heard the cedar tree speak to him. "My son," it said, "I will have pity on you. Because you do not want my power for yourself, but to do good for someone else, you shall have it. Always carry a sprig of cedar with you, hidden where no one else can see it, and never eat food that has been cooked over a fire of cedar wood. Those are the only rules I shall give you."

Drip Nose Boy was very tired and weak and hungry, and getting down the stone side of Mount Scott was hard, but he rested four times before he got to the bottom, and went on each time.

When he came to the village, Mountain Man was waiting for him. "Come to my tipi and let my wife cook you some broth," he said kindly.

Drip Nose Boy went with him, but before they came to the tipi he smelled the smoke of the cooking fire. It was cedar. He stopped where he was.

"Grandfather, I can't eat food cooked over that fire," he reported.

Grandfather took him by the hand and led him into the tipi. Drip Nose Boy was too tired to hold back. Inside the tipi he saw that the burning cedar was only a little incense flame, and that the real cooking fire was of oak. His grandmother sat beside it, helping Mountain Man's wife cook the broth.

"It is all right. He has succeeded," Mountain Man said to the women.

When Drip Nose Boy had drunk a little broth, Grandfather had a sweat lodge ready for him. He steamed himself and rubbed himself with sage and swam a little way in Medicine Creek. Then he lay down and slept, and when he woke Mountain Man had his work tools laid out for him, ready to begin to learn bow making.

All winter Drip Nose Boy worked learning to steam and bend the cedar, to scrape it smooth with a sharp piece of stone, to soak bands of sinew in water until they were soft, and then to bind them to the back of the bow to strengthen it. He learned to make bowstrings, and arrows, and to bind the arrows with owl feathers so that they would surely kill whatever they hit. Each time he bound the feathers to the arrows he took a sweat bath, so the owl power would not hurt him.

When spring came, Drip Nose Boy was ready. When the time came for the first spring buffalo hunt, Mountain Man lent him an old yellow horse. Drip Nose Boy rode out with the hunting party, but he hung behind them because he was ashamed of his poor clothes and his poor-looking horse.

But when they came in sight of the buffalo herd, it was different. That old horse remembered his hunting days, and he could run! Drip Nose Boy himself forgot how he looked, as he pulled an arrow from his quiver and set it to his bowstring. He rode with the best of them, and when they reached the herd, his arrow was the first one to bring a buffalo down. Because his grandmother was too old and weak to do much work, Drip Nose Boy had to skin and butcher the buffalo himself. He tied the meat in the skin and loaded it on his horse. That night he and his grandmother feasted on the ribs and the tongue of the buffalo.

In the morning, when the old lady was cutting up the meat to dry, some of the younger men came to see Drip Nose Boy.

"Where did you get that bow?" their leader asked.

"I made it," Drip Nose Boy said proudly.

"Could you make another? I will help you with the skinning and butchering if you will make me one like that."

"That would be good," Drip Nose Boy said.

The second bow was easier to make than the first, and each one he made after that was easier. One he traded for a horse of his own, but Mountain Man would not take back the old yellow horse. "He is yours. You keep him," he said. "If you want to make a return, bring me part of whatever animal you kill."

Soon Drip Nose Boy traded for many things; a captive woman to help his grandmother, a new tipi for them all to live in, and good clothes for them all to wear. People said he was a rich man, and they respected him for it.

Finally, Drip Nose Boy decided that the captive woman was kind and a good worker, and they were married. After that the people changed his name to Bow Man.

"You see," Mountain Man reminded him, "because you wanted nothing for yourself, everything has come to you."

Julia Berry, Kiowa-Apache

How the People Caught the Sun

KIOWA

The Kiowa of southwestern Oklahoma are, in many ways, a law unto
themselves. Their language us unrelated to that of any other American
Indians. In spite of the best efforts of linguists to align it with one or
another of the great linguistic stocks—Algonkin, Athabascan, Siouan,
Uto-Aztecan, Tewa, Keres, Yuman, or Penutian—Kiowa, linguisti-
cally, has not satisfactorily been classified.

To make matters worse, Kiowa originally was a tonal language, with
the meanings of many words depending on which of five pitches was
used in speaking them. Since 1930, two of the tones have been lost by
most speakers of Kiowa, and the remaining three are becoming increasingly blurred. One seldom hears "old Kiowa" spoken now except at
ceremonial gatherings and then only by the older people. It used to be
said that no non-Kiowa adult could learn to speak the language cor-
rectly, although children could, and this may well be true. Certainly
only a gifted musician, with an ear for absolute pitch, could have
learned it in its earlier form.

The Kiowa say that they came originally from the northwest, and
one of their origin myths centers around "Devil's Tower" in Wyoming. Many of their material culture traits also indicate a northern
origin: tall tipi poles like those used by the Crows; much emphasis on
men's hairdress, etc. Although the Kiowas got horses from the Comanches in the early eighteenth century, Kiowa women continued to breed

56

*dogs such as those used for travois-drawing and backpack loads almost
into the mid-twentieth century. Dog breeding was an important and
honored profession for Kiowa women, and it may be that their selective dog breeding led to the selective breeding of horses by men.*

*Physically, the Kiowa, both men and women, tend to be short and
stocky. Most families have some mixture of blood from Mexican captives, or from non-Indian captives taken in Texas or Kansas. Mous-
taches are not uncommon among Kiowa men. The women are quick
and active; polygamy was practiced into the twentieth century, and
the women frequently dominated their households. This was not surprising, because the men were often away on hunts or engaged in fighting.*

*Like many other American Indian tribes, the Kiowa have their
Trickster-Hero culture cycle of stories. Unlike their neighbors, the
Comanches, they do not have an animal Trickster, but a personified
one, Saynday. He is described as "funny-looking, very tall and thin,
with bulging arm and leg muscles, and a little moustache that hung
down over his mouth." The story that follows had been told by Alice
Marriott in a slightly different form in* Winter-Telling Stories, *published by T. Y. Crowell.*

*The telling of Saynday stories, whether they show him in his Tricks-
ter or his Hero manifestation, must always follow a fixed pattern of
opening and closing sentences.*

Saynday was coming along, but he had a hard time doing it. All his
world was dark, and he kept falling over things. At last he began to
get angry because the darkness made him clumsy, and just when he
was really losing his temper he bumped into his friends, Fox, Deer,
and Magpie. Magpie flew straight up in the air, and then came down,
but Fox and Deer were hurt when Saynday bumped them, and didn't
try to move.

"Look where you're going, can't you?" Fox demanded.

"It seems to me you could get along better than that," said Deer.

"Well try it yourselves and see how you make out," Saynday
snapped, and he sat down on the ground by a prairie dog hole. His
friends were tired of slipping and banging around, so they sat down
there with him.

"What we really need in this world is some light," Deer said, "I can't tell if I'm eating grass or weeds until I taste them. Sometimes the weeds taste nasty and make me sick."

"Well, at least you can find something to eat," snapped Fox. "How would you like it if you had to run after your food and catch it in the dark? The other day something I thought was a rabbit turned out to be a bear, and nearly ate me."

"What about you?" Saynday asked Magpie.

"Well," answered Magpie, "I can fly up in the air. When I get very high, I can see a little rim of light over in the east."

"There *is* light, then," said Saynday. "What we have to do is figure out a way to get it, so we can find our way around and be sure of what we're eating."

"Well, you figure it out," remarked Deer. "You're the one who's supposed to be smart."

The little prairie dog, by whose hole they were sitting, burrowed deeper in the earth. She was afraid that if Fox could see her he would eat her instead of a rabbit.

"Now, then," said Saynday, "if the light is so far away that Magpie can see only a little rim of it in the east, it will be too hard for one person to get it alone. We'll have to line ourselves up like a relay race. Fox, you can run hard and far. Go to the east, and get into the sun people's village. When you get to know them and they trust you, grab the sun and run. Deer can carry it next, and then Magpie. I'll put myself last, because you're all better runners than I am."

So Fox started on his journey to the east. At first he still stumbled around in blackness, but finally, ahead of him, he began to see the little rim of light on the edge of the world that Magpie had talked about.

The light grew and grew, ahead of Fox, and sometimes he had to stop and put his paws over his eyes, for fear it might blind him. When he did that he rested, too, to get ready for the big race.

At last Fox came to the sun people's camp, and he saw that they were playing a game. The men were lined up on two sides, and each side had four spears. First the leader on one side would roll the sun along the ground; then the opposite leader would. While the sun was rolling like a big ball, the men took turns with the spears trying to hit it. It was like the spear-and-hoop game the Kiowas still play.

Fox watched very quietly. One side was ahead, and when the losing side took their turns with the spears, Fox said, under his breath, so only their leader could hear him: "Good luck to the losers."

That time the losing side scored more points than the other, and again Fox wished them luck, and a third time when the score was even. When his side won, the leader came over to Fox, and asked, "Who are you, who wish us well and make us win?"

"Oh, I come from over there," said Fox pointing to the west with his puckered lips. "I'm one of old Uncle Saynday's boys."

"Never heard of him," said the sun camp man. "What are you doing here?"

"Just going along," said Fox, "trying to see the world." But he had to shut his eyes then, because the sun was so bright. (And you remember, a fox always sees well at night, and the sun is reflected in his eyes in the darkness.)

"Why don't you stay here a while?" asked the man. "You seem to be pretty lucky. We can teach you to play our game—if you promise to play on our side."

"All right," said Fox. "I'd like to learn the game."

Fox stayed in the sun camp for four months, and though he never did get used to the brightness, he did learn to play the spear game. When he got really good at it, and the game was going fast, Fox stabbed his spear into the sun, put it over his shoulder, and *ran*. He ran as hard and fast as he could, with the sun people right behind him.

Just as Fox was about to drop from running, he met Deer.

Deer grabbed the sun from Fox and ran as fast as he could, with the light growing and glowing all around him. The sun people weren't used to the darkness they were running into, and they began to slow down, but Deer didn't. He just tore along, and as he began to lose his breath, Magpie dived down out of the sky and grabbed the sun away from him. Now the other side of the world was getting darker and darker, and Saynday's side was becoming bright. When Magpie dropped down to the earth and gave the sun to Saynday, they had all the light there was in the world, but the sun was so hot it had burned black streaks on Magpie's feathers, which had been all white before.

Now the sun became a problem. Nobody knew what to do with it, and there was so much light all the time nobody could sleep except Fox, who was used to it.

"Maybe we'd better put it in the tipi," Saynday decided, "that way, it might not be so bright." But the tipi didn't seem to darken the sun enough.

"Put it on top of the tipi, so we don't have to look right at it," suggested Fox. But that was no good, because the sun set fire to the tipi and burned it right to the ground.

"Oh, throw it away," said Magpie, "it's just getting to be a nuisance."

"All right," Saynday agreed, "it's not worth the trouble we all went to to get it." And he picked up the sun and threw it into the sky. "Now stay there and travel around the world," Saynday ordered the sun. "Spend part of your time with the people on the other side, and part of it here with us." And he pushed the sun to the west to start it going around the world.

And that's the way it was, and that's the way it is, to this good day.

Frank Givvens, Kiowa

The inland ocean—the plains of North Dakota.

ABOVE Lodgepole pines were gathered in the Rocky Mountains, the Black Hills of South Dakota, and other places where the trees grew high, tall, and straight. They were cut as needed—when old tipi poles wore out or a new tipi was to be made for a bride; not at set intervals.

BELOW The great fields of the Dakotas are part of the inland ocean of the Plains, usually a rich and fertile area.

RIGHT AND BELOW Devil's Tower, Wyoming. This was a sacred place to many Plains Indian tribes, and is a part of their mythologies. The basalt pillars on the face are said to have been made by the claws of a bear, as it scrambled upward.

BELOW Wichita grass shelter, Anadarko, Oklahoma.

Wichita Mountains near Fort Sill, Oklahoma Territory, 1870s. *Soule photo, U.S. Army Field Artillery and Fort Sill Museum*

General Grierson's reconnaissance of Medicine Bluffs, 1868. (Grierson standing
on bank of bluff.) *Soule photo, U.S. Army Field Artillery and Fort Sill Museum*

ABOVE LEFT Pawnee buffalo robe, circa 1900. *Crane Collection, Denver Museum of Natural History*

ABOVE RIGHT Kiowa buffalo robe painted by James Auchia, 1972. Kiowa Indian. This robe represents the migrations and locations of Indian tribes throughout the United States. *U.S. Army Field Artillery and Fort Sill Museum*

BELOW Return of the buffalo, Wichita Mountains Forest Reserve, 1907. *U.S. Army Field Artillery and Fort Sill Museum*

Esse-too-yah-tay, a Penateka Comanche who guided General Grierson to Medicine Bluffs, December 1868. *U.S. Army Field Artillery and Fort Sill Museum*

Iowa man wearing modern "straight dance" costume.

Old Man Coyote and His Mother-in-Law

BRULÉ SIOUX

The following story was told by a completely acculturated person; a Bureau of Indian Affairs employee, and a well-educated man, in one of those storytelling sessions that take place around a table, after the second cup of coffee, while dinner is being digested. It was told as a hilarious joke, with somewhat naughty overtones.

Almost everywhere in the Plains tribes a man is rigidly forbidden to speak to his mother-in-law, to look at her, name her, except as "my wife's mother," or even to sit in the same tipi or room with her. The same taboo applies to a woman and her father-in-law, and also extends from the older persons to the younger ones. That it should have been told by a man to women was in itself a taboo violation.

Old Man Coyote makes trouble wherever he goes. He doesn't care what people think of him. He'll say and do anything.

One time his wife was away, visiting her sister. She left her mother behind to take care of Old Man and cook for him. The mother-in-law was very careful. She sat by the tipi door in the cooking place with her back turned to her son-in-law, and when she wanted to give him a bowl of food, she reached behind her and put it on the floor for him to pick up.

Well, this went on for about a week. Then a blizzard came up, and they had to stay in the tipi. Old Man Coyote was used to being out-doors and moving around and hunting, and he got bored. Finally he said, "I wish there was someone here to talk to." He looked right up at the tipi flaps when he said it.

"I feel the same way," the mother-in-law told the cooking fire.

So they sat there all day, looking up at the tipi flaps and staring into the cooking fire, and talked about all sorts of things. They told stories, and Old Man Coyote sang, but it sounded more like howling because his voice isn't very good any time.

"I wish he'd stop doing that," his mother-in-law remarked.

"It sounds worse than it is," Old Man Coyote replied, "because my voice is getting all strained from stretching my neck up."

"Well, why doesn't he look somewhere else?" the mother-in-law asked.

"I guess I can look at the fire," Old Man said, and he lowered his head and looked at the fire, and began to sing again.

"It isn't much better," his mother-in-law snapped.

"I sing better after I eat," said Old Man, so his mother-in-law got up and began to get their supper. When they sat down to eat, Old Man said, "I bet it would be easier sitting side-by-side, so she doesn't have to pass my food backwards to me."

So they sat side-by-side, their feet pointing at the fire, and ate their dinner together. When they had finished, Old Man took his little hand drum and began to sing again.

"That sounds a lot better," his mother-in-law said when she couldn't stand it any longer. "Maybe he'd better rest his voice, though. It's get-ting cold in here. We need some more firewood to get us through the night. Maybe he would go out and get us some wood."

So Old Man Coyote got up and went out and brought in a big load of firewood. He piled it up around the cooking place, and sat down again. "It certainly is getting cold," he said.

They talked some more, and then the mother-in-law began to yawn. "It's time for bed," she said, and began to lay out buffalo hides for Old Man Coyote to lie on. Then she made her own bed, and they both lay down.

"It's still too cold," Old Man said.

"Put another log on the fire," his mother-in-law told him, sleepily.

But even with a big blaze going, Old Man still complained about the cold. ''I'm used to having my wife to keep me warm in bed. You come over here. You're her mother, and you ought to be twice as warm as she is.''

His mother-in-law was tired of arguing and complaining, so she got up and got under his buffalo hide. As soon as Old Man began to snore, she slid out and put the largest log in the pile beside him, and went back to her own bed. When Old Man woke up in the morning, and saw what had been keeping him warm all night, the only thing he said— and he said it to the tipi flaps—was ''I hope my wife gets home soon.''

That's what happens to people who break the rules.

●━━━━■━━━━●

Storyteller's name withheld by request.

Old Man Coyote and Buffalo Power

SHOSHONI

Old Man Coyote is omnipresent among the Plains Indians. He is the universal trickster and troublemaker; probably the most annoying being on earth. Strangely enough, although coyotes in the buffalo days ran in packs, not, as they do now, living in single-family dens, Old Man is always represented as a loner; a one-to-himself character.

The story that follows is the Shoshoni version of one that is told the length and breadth of the Plains. It shows the Trickster-Hero in both his manifestations, good and bad.

Old Man Coyote was sitting out on a hillside, resting. He was just too tired to go anywhere else. He looked at himself. His skin was patchy and wrinkled, and his claws were worn down to the bone, and he could feel that there were almost no teeth left in his mouth.

"What am I going to do with myself?" Old Man wondered. "I can't hunt anymore, because I get short of breath when I run. If I did catch something I couldn't eat it, because I can't chew. What's going to happen to me? I used to have grandchildren I could depend on, but they've all run away and started families of their own."

He looked out across the prairies, and there stood a young, strong buffalo bull, with the sun shining on him and his head in the air, all proud and strong.

"My," Old Man thought, "I used to be just like that; I wish I could be again. Maybe he can help me."

He got up and hobbled down the hillside, and the buffalo just stood and watched, because he knew Old Man couldn't hurt him if he wanted to.

"What do you want?" the buffalo asked, when Old Man got pretty close to him.

"Huh? What you say?" Old Man Coyote said, putting his paw behind his ear so he could hear better.

"I said, what do you want?" the buffalo bull bellowed.

"Oh," said Old Man, "I don't want much. I just want to be young and strong again, like you. Buffaloes have all the power. They are everything for the poor Indians: food, shelter, clothes . . ."

"I know that," roared the buffalo. "Is that what you want? You want to be young and strong and beautiful?"

"Yes," answered Old Man, "and if anybody can do it for me, I know you can."

"I can do it," the buffalo told him, "but remember. If I do it, I am not giving you my power. You will look like a young strong buffalo, but you will still be Old Man Coyote inside. Don't ever forget that."

"I won't," Old Man promised.

"Then sit down there on the side of the mountain, and close your eyes," the buffalo directed. "Whatever you do, keep them closed until I tell you to open them."

"All right," said Old Man. He sat down on the south slope of the mountain and shut his eyes. The buffalo came running at him, and then he ran around Old Man. The first time Old Man kept his eyes shut tight, but the second time the buffalo stirred up so much dust, he sneezed and opened them.

"You've just about wrecked it," the buffalo complained. "I really was going to give you some power the fourth time around, but now you've spoiled things. Shut your eyes again, and I'll do what I can."

Old Man shut his eyes and put his paws over them. The buffalo ran around him again, and the fourth time he hit Old Man in the back, hard. They both tumbled down the side of the mountain, and when they got to the bottom, the buffalo said, "Now you can open your eyes."

Old Man opened them and looked at himself. He was a young, springy buffalo calf, all full of life.

"Thank you, my friend," he said to the buffalo, but the buffalo just snorted, and turned away. "I haven't got any time to play with youngsters," he said.

Well, for the next four years, Old Man really had himself a time. He was a young bull buffalo, growing up, and he felt wonderful. He ran and he wallowed in the shallow ponds, and he met a young buffalo woman, and made love to her. My, he was happy!

When the Calf-Coyote was full grown, he was running across the prairie, when he met a poor, old ragged coyote.

"Oh, help me, my friend," the old coyote said. "You have everything. Make me young and strong again, like you."

Calf-Coyote thought how sad the other one looked, and he forgot what the buffalo had told him when he became young again himself. "All right," he said. "I know how to do it. Come on to the Bear Butte with me."

So they went to the Bear Butte, very slowly, because the poor old coyote was just limping along. Sometimes Calf-Coyote got impatient and ran ahead, but the old coyote always called him back and asked for help, so he would slow down again because the other was so pitiful.

When they got to Bear Butte, Calf-Coyote showed the other just where to sit and told him to close his eyes. And he ran around and around him, twice, raising the biggest cloud of dust he could, until the other sneezed and opened his eyes.

"Now you've spoiled it," Calf-Coyote said, "but I'll try again and see what I can do."

So he ran around him twice more, and hit him in the back. They rolled down the side of Bear Butte, and when they got to the foot, there were two old hungry, poor Coyotes. You see Old Man had forgotten that the buffalo hadn't given him any power.

So always remember, don't start anything unless you know you can finish it.

Arthur Big Turnip, Shoshoni

Why Dogs Do Not Speak

KIOWA

As we have said before, the Trickster-Hero character is common to most American Indian tribes. The Kiowas, of the southern Plains, call him Saynday. Sometimes he does good things and sometimes he does bad ones, and his character illustrates the eternal duality of man.

Almost as pragmatic as the Comanches, the Kiowas believe that there is a reason for everything, and that if a thing works, it works. When there is no other explanation for any phenomenon they say "Saynday was coming along." He not only appears in the stories about the making of the world and the emergence of the Kiowas from underground and in the story of bringing the buffalo to feed his people but also in the "little stories" that explain why the animals and men are the way they are.

Although the Kiowas believe that when Saynday finished his work in this world, he left them, with only the print of his hand, the five bright stars of the Pleiades, to show that he was watching over them, Saynday is still very much alive in Kiowa thought and motivation.

Should you be wondering about such a trivial matter as why dogs do not speak, but communicate with their eyes and their tails, an old-time Kiowa would explain the matter in this way:

Saynday was coming along, and he came to the village where the dogs lived. Nah! They were all talking at once, and you never heard such a noise.

"Hush and be quiet," Saynday said. "I like to talk, too."

"We all know that," the father dogs growled. "We know it, too," the mother dogs barked, and even the little puppies yapped at him. All the dogs went right on talking.

"I tell you, be quiet," Saynday insisted, but the dogs paid no attention to him at all. Saynday began to get angry, but the madder he got the more the dogs growled and barked and yapped, harder than ever.

"This is about the last time," Saynday yelled. "If you don't hush up and listen to me, something bad will happen to you."

And still the dogs went on talking as loud as they could, and still Saynday got more and more angry. Finally he went and got his magic power things.

"I've warned you," he said to the dogs. "Don't say I didn't warn you. From now on none of you can say another word. You can growl and you can bark and you can yap when you need to, but nobody will understand you. From this day, you can only talk to people with your eyes and your tails."

And that's the way it was, and that's the way it is, to this good day.

Margaret Hunt Tsoodle, Kiowa

Why the Turtle's Shell
Is Checked

CHEYENNE

The Cheyenne belong to the Algonkian linguistic group, which occupied much of the area around the Great Lakes and east and west of the Mississippi River.

Like other members of the Algonkian family the Cheyenne were originally semisedentary people. They moved out onto the Plains, with the coming of the horse, in the seventeenth and eighteenth centuries. The horse made them a mobile people who could hunt more easily and wage war upon anyone who interfered with their movements.

The shift from a semisedentary horticulture-gathering economy to a subsistence based principally on hunting changed not only Cheyenne material culture but also, to some extent, social organization and mythological and religious beliefs. Although the change took place, the Cheyenne still retained in their mythology and religion many elements from the prehorse days.

Out on the Plains men became more economically important than women, as the hunters provided the buffalo that were the mainstay of Plains life. New men's societies developed not only to train the young men in hunting and war but also to give them the reassurance of the tribe. It was a period of shifting from a female ideology based on the Mother Earth to a male ideology based on the hunt and war.

Cheyenne social organization, like their mythology and religion, also retained remnants from the horticulture and gathering prehorse cul-

ture. It is generally assumed that a hunting society figures descent through the father, but this is not true of the Cheyenne. Descent was, and sometimes still is, figured through the mother's clan and family, although today a child will use its father's surname.

Children respected and recognized their father, but it was the mother's oldest brother who was responsible for their well-being. He shared the meat he got on the hunt with his sister's family, and, in turn, she skinned and butchered the animals he brought her, and tanned the skins. Mother's brother had a special relationship to his nieces and nephews, and they had a special name for him, while father's brothers were simply "fathers." The story that follows is probably from the pre-Plains culture, and shows the brother-sister relationship clearly.

The turtle is important in all Algonkian mythology, and so it is with the Cheyenne. Certain clans may make turtle-shaped cases to hold a piece of a baby's navel cord. The women of these clans hang the cases over the cradles so that the two parts of the baby will not be separated. Certain women fry bread in the shape of a turtle, and those who eat the bread receive a blessing. The significance of the particular animals chosen to accompany Turtle on the expedition described in this story is not known.

This is a Cheyenne "how and why" story. A little story to teach children with, but with serious overtones.

One time the animals were planning to go to war. There were Turtle, Skunk, Porcupine, Grasshopper, Snake, Cricket, and Willow who were going. They took Willow along to help them find water. Seven of them went on the war party.

So they started out, and in the evening they camped. Next morning, when the others were ready to start on again, Grasshopper had lost one of his legs, and had to stay behind. The others went on without him.

They were on the way all the second day, and that evening they camped again. Next morning when they got up, Cricket was singing, singing under a bush. He wouldn't come out when they called. So the others went on without him.

Now there were only five of them left. They were on their way all the third day, and that evening they camped again. In the morning,

Snake went down to the lake and went swimming, and when the others were ready to go on, he wouldn't come out. So they left him, and went on without him.

Now there were only four of them left. They were on their way all the fourth day, and that evening they camped again. They stayed all night close to a creek, and in the morning they got ready to start on again. Then they found that Willow had got stuck in the mud and couldn't pull loose. So the others left him there and went on.

Now there were only three of them left—Turtle, Skunk, and Porcupine. And that night, just at twilight, they came to the enemy village. They decided that they would raid it later on, after everybody was asleep. So, very carefully, when it was very dark, they sneaked into the chief's tipi, and before he could wake they scalped him to death. They cut his head off and took it away with them.

In the morning, when the people in the camp woke up, they found the chief lying there, with his head gone. They all cried and mourned, and hunted around, but they couldn't even find the tracks of the raiders.

Finally, one woman noticed a big wooden meat-pounding bowl turned over and upside down, and a little fine smoke coming out from under it. So she kicked the bowl and turned it over right side up, and there underneath it were the three enemy warriors with the chief's head. They'd already taken his scalp off, and were just getting ready to hold their victory dance.

Everyone came running out to see who had scalped the chief.

"Here they are!" all the people shouted. Porcupine grabbed up the scalp and ran away with it, and Skunk turned around and raised his tail and sprayed at the people, so everyone ran back and he got away with Porcupine. The only one left to be captured was poor little Turtle.

Then the enemy people began to wonder what they ought to do with their prisoner. And all the chiefs sat around and tried to decide, and Turtle shut himself up in his box. Sometimes he popped his head out and snapped at them.

That made the enemy people mad, and they decided to burn him. Some of the young men went off to get the wood to make up a great big fire. When they had brought in stacks of branches they built the fire up, while poor Turtle just sat on the ground and blinked at them.

After the fire was burning up high, the people picked Turtle up and threw him on it. He stretched out his legs and kicked around, and kicked all the wood away, so he was out of danger, but his shell was all cracked and checked from the heat.

So the people wondered again what to do with Turtle, and finally they decided to drown him. Then he pretended to get all nervous and shaky, and begged them not to do it. But still they wanted to drown him, and to have a big dance to celebrate their victory.

The enemy chief said, "Turtle, have you got anything to say before you die?"

Turtle was crying and sobbing. "Yes," he wept. "I want to die like a man."

"That's the way to do it," the chief said. "Die like a man whenever you can. Now, what do you want to say to us?"

"Well," sobbed Turtle, "this is my last request. Let all my sisters know I died like a man. I want two of your biggest chiefs to take me down to the river and put me in the water."

"Oh, that's fine," said the head chief. "Two chiefs are the very ones that will do it."

So two young war chiefs took Turtle, one on each side of him, and hauled and shoved him down to the river, and he hung back and cried and begged every step of the way. But they took him down to the water and put him in, and dragged him out to the middle of the river before they turned him loose. When the two young men were in the water up to their waists, Turtle suddenly grabbed them and pulled them under, and drowned them both.

The people on the bank saw what had happened, but they were afraid to go in the water and bring Turtle out. But one old lady had a good idea. She told the people to go back to camp and get their bowls and buckets, so they could bail all the water out of the river.

The people worked all day, but they couldn't seem to get the river dry. After dark they gave up and went back to camp for a rest. Then Turtle dragged the two young chiefs out of the water and up on the bank, and scalped them both. He cut their heads off, too, although they were dead already. Then he started home with his two scalps.

Just before Turtle got home to his village, Porcupine and Skunk came in with their one scalp. Everybody was excited about their success, and the announcer went around hollering, so you could hear him way out on the prairie, "That's the way to be a man! Look at Porcupine and Skunk! Porcupine and Skunk!"

Then Turtle came quietly home to his tipi, where his sister was sitting weeping because he hadn't come back. Oh, she was so glad to see him, when he came in carrying his two scalps. And while they were talking to each other, the crier came around again, naming Porcupine and Skunk. Then Turtle's sister, Miss Turtle, ran out with her two scalps and sang,

> My brother Turtle,
> He's a man, too,
> Right along with these others,
> He's got scalps.

"Shut up, Old Wrinkle Legs, and come back in here. I'm mad!" Turtle yelled out at her.

So Miss Turtle came back in the tipi and asked her brother what was the matter.

"I did the hard work of getting that scalp they're carrying around, and now I've brought in two more, but their bands haven't named me once. Go and tell our Turtle band I want war with those bands."

So the word got around the camp, and Skunk and Porcupine got scared. They came outside the tipi and called, "Turtle! Turtle! That's the way to be a man! We heard you brought in two more scalps. We're going to have a big victory dance for you!"

Then Turtle cheered up, and went out where his sister was crying about the names he called her. Like all lady turtles, Maheo, the Creator, had given her beautiful leggings with yellow stripes, while to the man turtles he had given red ones, and she didn't like being called Old Wrinkle Legs.

"Sister," Turtle called, "who told you to cry? I went to war to bring you happiness. I fought hard. See—my shell is all cracked and checked from the heat of the fire the people threw me into. But it was worth it to make you happy. Dry your eyes and go and get ready to dance with these two scalps."

So his sister jumped up, happy once more. "Oh, Brother Turtle! Brother Turtle!" she cried. So she ran back to the camp and danced, and they were all peaceful and happy.

That's why we always say Turtle was so smart, and we give him to children to wear, so they will grow up the same way.

Mary Little Bear Inkanish, Cheyenne

Why the Prairie Dogs' Tails Are Short

KIOWA

We could almost call this story intertribal, for it is told with variations the length and breadth of the Plains.

It was the first Saynday story one of us ever heard, and the telling was in another context: How a little boy of six, around 1900, begged his father, on the way to the trading post, to stop the wagon beside a prairie dog town. He got down and danced solemnly around, singing the Saynday song, and the wise little prairie dogs scuttled into their holes like the last one in the story.

The charming picture of a square, solid little brown boy dancing up and down beside the mounds that covered the ground rodents' intricately constructed subterranean warrens, has remained with the listener ever since. It is matched by the accompanying picture of the indulgently smiling parents, high on the wagon seat, watching the performance.

Saynday is as much alive to Kiowa children today as he was at the turn of this century. Children at a school in Carnegie, Oklahoma, asked us to tell them Saynday stories when we visited the school in 1973. Once in a while a small hand shot up in the third-grade room, and we were informed that Grandmother told a particular story differently. But there were no complaints about the prairie dog story.

Saynday was coming along, and he began to feel hungry. Of course, the only times when Saynday *didn't* feel hungry were while he was eating something. He was like that, if he didn't get into trouble, he got hungry.

"Well," Saynday said to himself, "I guess I'd better get something to eat. I wonder what there is around here?"

Saynday looked around, but he couldn't see anything to eat at first. The birds were flying too high in the sky, and he had forgotten his bow and arrows, so he couldn't shoot a buffalo or a deer. It was too early in the spring for wild berries, and there weren't any berries around anyway. Saynday was hungry enough to eat a fish or a snapping turtle, but there wasn't any water, either.

Then he looked along the ground at his feet, and he saw a prairie dog town. In those days all the prairie dogs had long tails, like real dogs, and they were frolicking around outside their houses, playing tag, and chasing each other. They really looked like the ground squirrels they are, in those days.

"That's fine!" Saynday said out loud, still talking to himself, "there's nothing better than a good mess of prairie dog stew. Now, how am I going to catch them?"

He looked around and looked around, and at last he found a stick. It wasn't a very big stick, but it was big enough to kill prairie dogs with. Saynday walked over to the prairie dog town, using his stick like a cane, and stood and watched them play.

"Good morning, Saynday," said the prairie dog chief. "What's on your mind today?"

"Oh, I was thinking," Saynday replied. "Just walking along and thinking. I was catching a song."

"Is it a good song?" asked the prairie dog chief.

"I'm not sure yet," Saynday answered. "I like it, but maybe you wouldn't."

"Let us hear the song," the chief said.

But Saynday told him, "There's a dance that goes with it. Everybody has to dance, and maybe everybody doesn't feel like dancing."

"Oh, yes!" all the prairie dogs said together.

And Saynday shook his head and said, "Everybody has to take part, or it won't be right."

"Come on, Saynday," said the prairie dog chief. "Be a man. Show us your dance and sing us your song, so we can learn it. Don't be selfish and keep it all for you."

"Oh, all right," Saynday said. "If you really want to learn it, I'll teach you."

"That's fine!" exclaimed all the prairie dogs.

"Well," said Saynday, "first we all make a big circle, clear around your village."

So the prairie dogs made a line, circling the village and facing inward, toward the mounds on top of their houses.

"Now we all join hands," Saynday instructed them.

So Saynday and the prairie dogs all joined hands, all the way around the circle.

"Now dance sidewise, to your left," said Saynday. "This is going to be called a round dance."

All the prairie dogs stood with their left feet ready to step sidewise, and Saynday began to sing:

> Prairie dogs, prairie dogs,
> Wag your tails.
> *Now* is the time to dance the best.
> *Now* is the time to dance the best!

And every time he said "*now*" Saynday jumped up in the air, and the prairie dogs tried to jump up, too, but they couldn't, because their bodies were round and their hind legs were short.

They sang and danced around in a circle four times, and all the prairie dogs said, "Oh, that was fine, Saynday. Let's do it again!"

"Do you really want to?" Saynday asked doubtfully.

"Oh, yes!" the prairie dogs shouted in their chattery voices. "That's a fine dance. It's fun."

"Well, let's try it a different way, then," Saynday said. "Shut your eyes, and see if you can dance without opening them."

So the prairie dogs shut their eyes, and Saynday began to sing again,

> Prairie dogs, prairie dogs,
> Wag your tails.
> *Now* is the time to dance the best.
> *Now* is the time to dance the best.

As soon as all the prairie dogs had their eyes closed, Saynday joined the hands of the two he was holding, and picked up his stick. While the prairie dogs danced around in front of him, Saynday kept on singing, but everytime he said "*now*" he hit one of the prairie dogs on the head with his stick, and put that one aside for his dinner. He kept on singing and hitting, until all but one of the prairie dogs was killed. She was an old wise one at the end of the line, and she opened her eyes just as Saynday raised his stick for the last time. Quick as a flash, the prairie dog ran into the hole, but Saynday's stick came down on the end of her tail and cut it off short.

"I'll let you go," said Saynday. "If I don't, there won't be any more prairie dogs. But from now on you will all have short tails, and you will always have one man prairie dog sitting up on his mound, to watch out and guard the village."

And that's the way it was, and that's the way it is, to this good day.

George Hunt, Kiowa
A different version of this story was told by Alice Marriott in Winter Telling Stories, *Thomas Y. Crowell, N.Y., 1969.*

PART 3

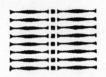 Horseback Days

The Magic Dogs

COMANCHE

The Comanche of the southern Plains have been described as natural pragmatists and natural skeptics. Shoshonean-speaking, they probably came from the northwest in the great southward migration that took place between A.D. 500 and A.D. 1200. The first wave of Shoshoneans settled the Hopi villages of northern Arizona. The Comanche probably represented a second movement, since their language is mutually intelligible with the northern Shoshoni proper, but not with Hopi.

The Comanche have always been resistant to outsiders. Their only known allies were the Kiowas and Kiowa-Apaches, and those alliances never lasted for very long.

The Comanches raided as far north as the Black Hills of South Dakota, Wyoming, and as far south as Sonora. Stripped to breechclout and moccasins, their men took captives wherever they went, even before the horseback days, prior to the last half of the 1600s. It might be safe to say that no such thing as a pureblood Comanche has existed for centuries.

Great braggarts, tricky gamblers, fearless, handsome people, they had great dash and courage. Yet Comanches are not without humor, and they have their own code of honor. Polygamy was common among them; they had no clan system, but brothers did marry their brothers' or cousins' widows.

In the old days, the people walked wherever they went. They had to. They had dogs to pull or carry their loads, but no horses. Then one day a man came out of the brush-covered tipi that belonged to his second wife, and looked to the west. He saw a herd of strange animals coming along. They were almost as big as buffalo, with long necks and tails, and humps on their backs. The man called to his wives, ''Come here and see these things.''

Everybody in the village came out, and they all stood and stared. The herd came closer, and they could see that the humps were shiny, and looked hard—as hard as stone. It was a very strange sight.

When the herd came up to the village, the dogs ran out, barking and trying to drive them off, but the strange animals kicked at them with their hind feet, or reared up and tried to strike the dogs with their front feet. Those were terrible feet, covered with the same shiny hard stuff as the humps.

''Wah!'' said one Comanche man. ''This is very strange, indeed.''

Then a voice spoke from the hump of the leading animal.

''Quien es? (Who are you?)'' it said, in a man's voice.

The Comanches shook their heads, and some of the women drew back into their brush tipis, taking the children with them, because they were afraid. Even the men were afraid, because the animal suddenly split itself in two. The hump got down off the creature's back, and stood on the ground like a man. It was magic; all magic, because when the hump got down, the rest of the animal, with four legs on the ground, looked like a huge dog. The magic dogs!

The man opened his mouth and pointed down his throat with his finger. The Comanches waited to see what would come out. Nothing did, and they shook their heads. Then the man rubbed his stomach with one hand and worked his jaws as if he were chewing.

''I guess he wants food,'' said a Comanche woman, who was peering out of her tipi.

''What do you think he eats?'' her husband asked.

''Meat and bones, like a dog?'' the woman wondered. But just then the lower part of the animal lowered its head to the ground, and began to eat the grass that was growing there.

''He wants grass,'' her husband remarked. ''Send the children to get him some.''

So the women sent their children out to gather grass, and they put a great pile of it in front of the creature. The lower part ate the grass, but the upper part still signed that it was hungry.

"Bring him some meat and bones," the husband ordered, and the woman did, but the strange being wouldn't eat the raw meat and bones. He shook his head at them, and pointed to the cooking fires.

"He wants it cooked," the woman said. Then two or three other animals separated themselves, and came over to the Comanches.

"Nosotros estan Español," they said. "Carne cocido, por favor." ("We are Spanish. Cook it, please.")

So all the women in camp got busy. They already had dug cooking holes in the ground and lined them with rawhides. Their cooking stones were heating in the camp fires. As fast as they could, they cut up deer meat and dropped it in the holes, and poured in water. By that time, the stones were red hot, and the women lifted them out of the fires with sticks and dropped them in the water. Pretty soon the stews began to steam and smell good.

When the stews were cooked. the women handed horn spoons to the strangers, who were all sitting around on the ground, and motioned them to eat. They had to dip their food out of the holes, because the Comanches in those days had spoons, but no bowls. But the new people managed all right. They took bowls from the backs of the magic dogs, and dipped out the stew and ate it like men.

When everybody had eaten, including the Comanches, the first man laid his face on the palm of his hand and closed his eyes, to show that he was sleepy. The Comanches gave them hides to lie on, and pretty soon all the newcomers were asleep.

"What shall we do?" asked one of the war chiefs.

"We could kill them, and take their magic dogs. That's what I'd like, to own a magic dog."

"No," said a very old man, who was wise in counseling. "Don't kill them. You wouldn't know what to do with a magic dog if you had one. Follow them when they leave here, and watch how they take care of the dogs. Then you will know better."

But the strangers didn't seem in any hurry to go. They stayed four days, and the one who seemed to be their leader, whom the others called "Don Francisco" or "Mi Capitán" made signs to the Comanches when they all wanted food. He even took his men down to the river, where they took off their hard shiny outer skins, and went swimming. Under the outer skins they were white all over, as if they had been sick a long time.

Their muscles looked strong enough, even if their arms and legs were covered with hair. That was almost as surprising to the Comanches as the first sight of the Spaniards had been, and it disgusted them, too, because the Comanche people have almost no hair on their bodies and faces. But of course they were used to taking sweat baths and rubbing themselves all over with sage, and the wise old man said that was probably why they had so little hair, compared with these others.

After the Spaniards had bathed, they put on some soft-looking clothes and got ashes from the cooking fires. They didn't even ask the women if they could have the ashes; they just took them. Then they rubbed and rubbed the hard stuff until it was shinier than ever. Oh, they were very strange people!

At the end of the four days, the Spaniards rode out of the Comanche camp toward the west. The Comanche war chief waited until noon time, and then he led his party after them.

It was easy to follow their trail; they didn't try to wipe it out in any way. The Comanches had long trailers on the heels of their moccasins that swished back and forth as they walked, and wiped out the footprints. But the prints and the dung of the magic dogs made a trail nobody could have missed.

They went out onto the flat plain, and around the canyons that broke it here and there, and they traveled a long way, from water hole to water hole. The Comanches broke off yucca stalks and thrust them in the ground to stake the back trail.

All the time, the Comanches watched. They saw that at night time the Spaniards took big pads off the dogs' backs, and the ropes they held to guide them off their heads. Then the men took the horses to a water hole to drink, and let them roll on the ground and shake themselves all over before they ate any grass. At night, they tied the horses' legs together with strips of rawhide, so they could go jumping around camp, but could not run away. When morning came, the Spaniards returned the big pads to the horses' backs, and took off the rawhide bindings from their legs, and put the ropes back on their heads. They did these same things every day.

At first the war chief thought he could sneak into the camp at night and take a horse, but the Spaniards took turns guarding, so there was never a good chance to get at the horses. Finally, late one evening, they went through a pass in the mountains that had been growing up in the west, ahead of them. These were the biggest mountains the Comanches had ever seen—a lot bigger than the Wichitas or the Guadalupes.

Beyond the mountains was a wide river, and when they had forded it, there was an Indian village. It was built of mud and stone, not out of grass like the Wichita houses the Comanches had seen, and this village was square, not round like a camp circle. It made a solid wall around an open space, but the Spaniards did not take their horses inside the wall. Instead, they turned the horses out in a little grassy place. Then they went inside the wall. Everything beyond the river was barren desert. The horses had to stay where they could eat.

Late at night the Comanche war chief slipped up to the grassy spot. The horses were not frightened because they had gotten used to the Comanche smell by that time. The war chief had brought along the braided rawhide rope his wife used when she was gathering firewood, and he put it over a horse's head, and led him away. Then another man did the same thing.

They followed their own backtrail across the broken plains, going from one stake to the next, until they were back in their own village south of the Wichita Mountains. There they learned to ride the horses bareback, but because one horse was a stallion and the other a gelding, they did not mate, and so when they died, the Comanches ate them. They knew they would have to get a female some way, but it was a long time before they did. Then they went north, up the river, to a place where another joined it, and found many Spaniards and horses. The Comanches came away that time with mares and stallions, and now they could breed them. Then other Indians came and traded with the Comanches for their horses, and the Comanches became famous riders and raiders.

* * *

The incident of the Spaniards who came to the Comanche camp, bathed, and helped themselves to the women's ashes was told by Jean Edwards, Comanche, who had heard it from her grandmother. The rest has been compiled from accounts of the Coronado expedition and the Oñate settlement at San Juan Pueblo.

Out of the Earth Houses

CHEYENNE

Again we turn to the Cheyenne. Originally earth lodge people, the Cheyenne retained the form of the lodge in their Sun Dance. A large circular enclosure, it was constructed with an upright center pole and a circle of other uprights surrounding it.

All the bands of any one tribe gathered together for the Sun Dance, each camping in its appointed place in a great circle. An open space was left on the east round of the ring, as if the ring were a tipi, which must always face east, except at this time, when all tipis were turned inward, facing the Sun Dance lodge.

There were four days of preparation for the Sun Dance. A center pole was chosen (usually by the peace chiefs), cut down, and carried reverently into camp. The bark had to be stripped from the pole, and then the Sun Dance priest, the guardian of the Sun Dance bundle, painted two red and two black strips on the pole. A hole was dug, and the pole set in the earth and stamped in place, with two forked branches at the top. People tied their offerings to the pole, and in some cases a part of a medicine bundle was also fastened to it. Every ceremonial action had to be preceded by three attempts before it could be completed on the fourth attempt.

These first four days were days of celebration, feasting, meeting, and greeting friends, and going out to gather the secondary poles and the brush or willows that would thatch the lodge. This was a period of ceremonial license; men and women went out together to gather brush, and it was considered a great joke if a woman rode with her brother-

in-law, since he was a potential husband already. There was a great deal of flirting and courting, marriages were arranged and sometimes anticipated, and gifts were given to old people and to visitors from other tribes.

At the end of the fourth day, the whole mood changed. The men who had pledged that they would dance, either to ask for blessings or to give thanks for their families, led by the Sun Dance priest and accompanied by sponsors—older men who had danced four Sun Dances— filed into the lodge and seated themselves on beds of sage. The sponsors painted the sacred designs on the dancers' bodies, hung eagle wing bone whistles around their necks, and instructed them. The singing began to the accompaniment of rawhide rattles—usually made from buffalo scroti—beaten on a rolled-up piece of rawhide. Any man who was not dancing was free to take part in the singing, and sometimes women sang with them.

The first dance began. The dancers took their whistles between their teeth, fixed their eyes on the center pole, and began a rhythmic rising on their toes and falling back on their heels, while they blew the whistles. From the time the vowers went into the lodge until they came out, four days later, they might neither eat nor drink.

The dance ended at sunset of the eighth day. The Sun Dance priest took a fan made from eagle wing feathers in some tribes, from raven wing feathers in others, and chased the dancers around the lodge and out of it in each of the four directions. After that, the vowers were released, and went to their family camps, where they were given a small amount of water and some broth, as if they had returned from a vision quest as, in fact, they had. Sun Dance visions were not uncommon.

Variations from tribe to tribe are endless, but one rule seems to have held true everywhere. A man must dance in four Sun Dances to receive the full blessing. In some tribes, a torture element was mandatory for the dancers. The men slit the skin over the pectoral and cervical muscles, inserted wooden skewers, and either roped themselves to the center pole or hung stones or buffalo skulls from the skewers. The idea was to pull back from the pole, or to go through the camp with the heavy burden until the skewers pulled through the skin and freed the dancer. One of the authors still recalls, with a shudder, the scars some of the old men with whom she worked with could show. It was because of the self-torture that the government banned the Sun Dance in the late 1800s.

Maheo was the one who made the world and the people and animals
and wind and stars. He was the one who brought the light and divided
night from day. Maheo, the All Spirit, watched over his people, the
Cheyenne, and taught them everything.

One day the Comanches came to see the Cheyennes. The Comanches
were riding on horses. "Wah! That is wonderful," said the Cheyennes. "Where do you get them?"

"From the Pueblos," the Comanches said. "They have lots of
horses."

"What do you trade for them?" asked the Cheyennes. Their own
women made many pretty things, decorated with earth paints and porcupine quills that they dyed with the earth colors and berry juices, but
they knew the Comanches did not do that kind of work.

"Trade for them!" said the Comanches, laughing. "We don't trade
for them. We just go and take them."

"Don't the Pueblos get angry?" asked the Cheyennes.

"Oh, they don't like it very much, but they're too afraid to go out
of their houses to come and get them back."

"We never heard of horses," said one Cheyenne priest. "Perhaps
Maheo wouldn't like for us to have them."

"Why don't you ask him?" a Comanche said. "We'll trade with
you, if you're too afraid to go and get them."

The Cheyennes knew that was true because the Comanches enjoyed
taking great risks. They were gamblers, who were always looking for
things to put at stake in their lives or their games.

The Cheyenne priests all gathered in the largest house in the village,
which was the medicine lodge, and they sat and smoked and prayed to
Maheo, fasting, for four days. At last Maheo took pity on them, and
spoke to them through the oldest priest.

"You may have horses," Maheo said. "You may even go with the
Comanches and take them. But remember this: If you have horses
everything will be changed for you forever.

"You will have to move around a lot to find pasture for your horses.
You will have to give up gardening and live by hunting and gathering,
like the Comanches. And you will have to come out of your earth
houses and live in tents. I will tell your women how to make them, and
how to decorate them.

And there will be other changes. You will have to have fights with
other tribes, who will want your pasture land or the places where you

hunt. You will have to have real soldiers, who can protect the people. Think, before you decide."

The priests sat and smoked and thought another four days. Then the oldest one said, "Maheo, we think we can learn the things you can teach us and our women. We will take the horses, and with your guidance we will learn the new life."

"So be it," said Maheo. "But you must never forget where you came from or who you are. Once a year you must make a lodge in the shape of an earth lodge, and in it you must pray and dance and smoke and sing. It will be your offering of your own flesh and blood in my honor."

All the priests agreed. Then Maheo said, "I will give the power of this dance to the oldest of you, and he can pass it on. But because women are the mothers of life, as I am the father of everything, it must be passed through a woman. On the third night of the dance, the priest must take the wife of a man who is making offerings into a special tipi, set aside, and lie with her. Then she will lie with her husband, and the power will be passed through her body to his."

"People will say ugly things about us if we do this," the priests protested.

"Nobody can say anything ugly about something sacred," Maheo told them. "This will not be just any woman. She must be known to be true to her husband, to care for her children and her home, and to make fine quillwork. There shall be a society of such women. If any of them is ever untrue to her husband, she must be put out of camp. Now call the women together, and I will talk to them."

So the crier went up on the roof of the earth lodge, and called, "All you women, came here. Listen to what Maheo is going to tell you."

So Maheo spoke to the women. "You must make special tipis if you belong to this society. They will have bands of quillwork on them, red and yellow and black, all the colors alternating in each of twenty-eight stripes, and with a tuft of red buffalo hair on each yellow patch. Then make pillows and bedspreads and tipi linings and robes for your little girls in the same pattern.

"If a woman wants to honor her son-in-law, and show respect for him, she should make him a tipi like that, and a pair of striped moccasins in the same pattern, and a saddle blanket. Then she can put these things on her best horse and take it to her son-in-law, and give it all to him. Then they can sit down and eat together, and talk to each other, like a real mother and son. Otherwise they must stay away from each other in every way; not even to speak each other's names.

"But remember, you women. This is hard work. You must not do it when you are not well, or when there are any men around. If even a baby boy comes near you, your work will be spoiled. The night before you start one of these things you must take a sweat bath. Then get up with the sun and work until it sets. Some women won't want to take all that trouble. That's all right. But when you finish, and hold a feast of thanksgiving, those women may not eat with you."

Just as Maheo said, some women agreed to follow his instructions, but others were afraid. Then Maheo gave the women who agreed a bundle with quills from the north, and sinew and awls and a pipe in it, and told them to smoke four times during the day when they were working, like men on a power quest.

After all this was done, the Cheyenne came out of the earth lodges and said to the Comanches, "It's all right. Maheo says we may go with you or trade with you and learn to live the way you do."

The Comanches stayed with the Cheyennes another four days, and their women showed the Cheyenne women what kind of wood to use for tipi poles, and how to cut and sew a tipi, and how to tie the poles to their horses, and load them with the tipis and the other things they needed. "We will let the old people and the little children ride on the poles," the Cheyennes decided.

Then they put up the center pole, and built the lodge-above-ground and held their first Sun Dance. They called it The Standing Against the Enemy Dance, because the hot summer sun burned down on them. But the Comanches rode away, because their power was horse-catching, not dancing. The Cheyennes were glad they left, and did not see the first transfer of power, so the Comanches could not talk about it.

The Cheyennes still hold the Sun Dance, in the north in July, and in the south in August. If a man pledges to dance in the Sun Dance, he must do so for four years. All the people tie their best things to the center pole for offerings, and some of the men make offerings of flesh and blood. The Sacred Woman sits in the tipi with the priests, and fasts with the dancers the whole four days while the other men, who are not dancing, sing. This is the way the Cheyennes do sacred things.

Belle Martin, Cheyenne

The Bear Butte

CHEYENNE

The Bear Butte stands north of Lame Deer, Montana, on the road to Forsyth. It is a sandstone monolith, its sides deeply scarred and eroded, so sand is piled at its foot. It has been a sacred place to the Cheyennes for centuries. Men still scramble up its eastern face, and from the top, a hundred feet or more above the valley floor, they watch the sun rise four successive times, praying and fasting and smoking in their search for power.

If you go to the Bear Butte, you must take an offering of tobacco with you. Cigarettes are all right, if that's all you have, but loose tobacco is better. Stand on the east side of the butte and pray for mercy and protection, while you scatter the tobacco to the four world corners. Then look on the ground at your feet. If your prayers are to be answered you will find a token, perhaps a white bead, or a quartz arrow point. Then you will know that your life will always be blessed by Maheo, the Above Spirit. This is the story the Cheyennes tell of the Bear Butte.

Once there was a very beautiful young woman. Her father was a chief, who was a wise guardian for his people. He had no son, but he had many horses, and lots of young men came to ask him for his daughter. He always said no.

A Crow man came, walking proud and handsome, his long hair trailing on the ground behind him, as if he owned the earth.

"Give me your daughter," he said to the chief.

"No," the father answered, "she must stay with her own people."

The Crow man went away, shaking his head, and very angry.

"I don't want a Crow to cut your hair off and paste it to his own to make himself look more handsome," said the chief to his daughter. "You are too beautiful to be treated like that."

Next came a Sioux man, with his great crested war bonnet standing up straight on his head, and his nose hooked and pointed down, as if he smelled something bad.

"Give me your daughter," he said. "I have three wives all ready, and I promise you she will not have to work."

"No," said the father, "she is a good worker, and while I prize her, I want her to work. Otherwise she will become fat and lazy."

"Have it your own way," said the Sioux, and he got on his horse and rode off, never looking back.

"That is no life for a young healthy woman," said the chief. "You shall stay here with me until the right man comes along."

Next came a white man, loaded with traps and furs, and with a little keg on his back. "I hear you have a daughter for sale," he said to the chief.

"She is not for sale," the father answered. "I certainly would not give her to you."

"I will give you all my skins."

"No. I can catch better ones myself."

"I will throw in all these traps, with the skins."

"No. She is not for sale."

"I will throw this in, too," said the trapper, juggling the keg on his back so that it gurgled.

"Go away," the chief shouted, "do you think I would trade my daughter for that stuff that makes men crazy? She is too good and proud for that!"

So the trapper went off into the mountains, and nobody ever saw him again.

At last a very tall, handsome young man, dressed like a Cheyenne, came.

"I am looking for a wife," he said.

"That's better," the chief snorted. "All the others just said, 'Give

Satanta's daughter, Sah-tope-ay-doh, Pipe Holder, and brave. *U.S. Army Field Artillery and Fort Sill Museum*

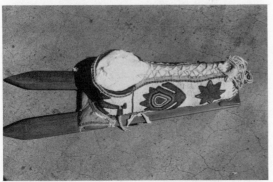

TOP LEFT Cheyenne woman's jewelry—necklace and cartridge case bracelets. The bracelets were made after the Civil War from Howitzer shell casings. *Marriott Collection*

TOP RIGHT Cheyenne women's elk horn scraper with metal edge. The metal blade was used to clean flesh from the hide. Before the Indians obtained metal, a stone blade was used. The scraper is used by a standing woman, like a hoe. *Denver Art Museum*

LEFT Kiowa cradle. This is a horseback cradle, made so that if it falls from the pommel, the child will be protected whatever position it lights in. *U.S. Army Field Artillery and Fort Sill Museum*

BELOW LEFT Ute beaded bag, made about 1950. Used to show influence of acculturation. *Marriott Collection*

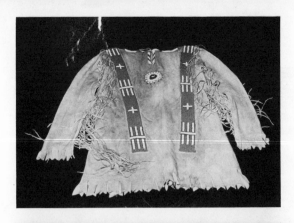

TOP AND RIGHT Cheyenne boy's beaded and fringed shirt. Sun disk design on front (top) and back (right). *Denver Art Museum*

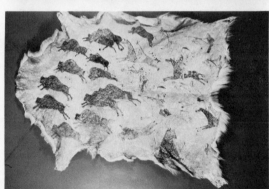

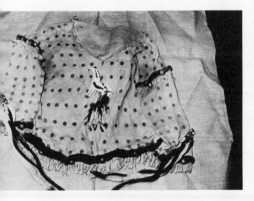

ABOVE LEFT Blackfoot "bulletproof" shirt (front). The "protection" comes from the painted designs, and is spiritual (or magical, or shamanistic). *Denver Art Museum*

ABOVE RIGHT Tanned deerskin pictograph depicting a hunt with Buffalo Bill. Painted deerskin probably from Standing Rock Reservation. Earth colors on soft-tanned buckskin, circa 1900. *Norman Paulson, North Dakota State Historical Society*

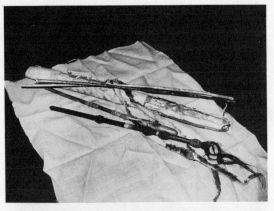

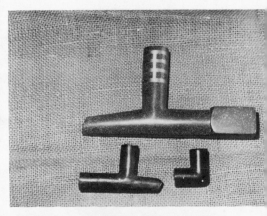

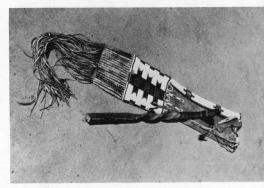

TOP LEFT Crow Indian medicine kit and painted rawhide case. *Denver Art Museum*

TOP RIGHT Cheyenne pipes. The top pipe is made of Catlenite and trimmed with German silver. It was made in the 1960s by one of the last living Northern Cheyenne pipe makers. *Marriott-Rachlin Collection*

ABOVE LEFT Plains peyote equipment. *Marriott-Rachlin Collection*

ABOVE RIGHT Cheyenne pipe case, made for a man's everyday pipe. *Marriott-Rachlin Collection*

ABOVE LEFT Arapaho dice game. The dice are tossed in the basket, and the score depends on the number of similar faces turned up. The dice in this set are wild plum pits, and the basket is made of yucca. It is plaited, *not* woven. *Marriott-Rachlin Collection*

ABOVE RIGHT Cheyenne medallion. These are very fashionable and popular ornaments at present. This was made by Mary Inkanish, Cheyenne. *Marriott-Rachlin Collection*

BELOW RIGHT Carved Cheyenne wooden buffalo used ceremonially in Sun Dance. *Philbrook Art Museum, Tulsa, Oklahoma*

BELOW LEFT Cheyenne Sun Dance figures. Used for their spiritual value in the Sun Dance. *Crane Collection, Denver Museum of Natural History*

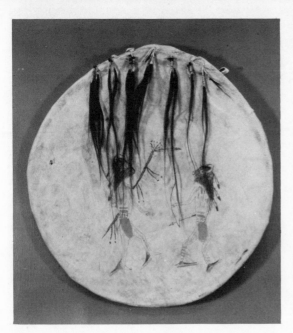

ABOVE LEFT Buckskin shields like this one were carried by buffalo dancers of many tribes. On this shield the artist has drawn two men dancing the buffalo dance. *Norman Paulson, North Dakota State Historical Society*

ABOVE RIGHT Arapaho Dragonfly shield. Trailer turned back. Dragonflies are associated with water, so this shield probably had water power. *Denver Art Museum*

BELOW LEFT Comanche painted quiver case. Earth colors on rawhide. *Denver Art Museum*

BELOW RIGHT Trade tomahawk with brass saddler's studs and Crow beaded buckskin wrist and strap pendant. The use of saddler's tacks is evidence of acculturation. *Denver Art Museum*

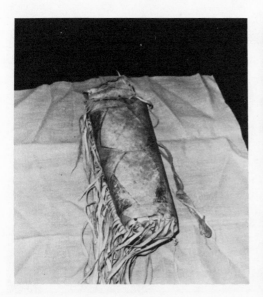

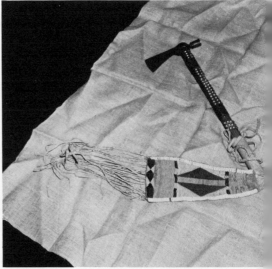

ABOVE LEFT Cheyenne rawhide case (parfleche). Earth paints on rawhide. These cases, which could be packed flat on a dog, or horse or in a travois, were used to carry clothing, dried food, and other necessities. At night in the tipi they served as pillows and backrests. *Denver Art Museum*

ABOVE RIGHT Blackfoot man's leggings made of trade cloth. Beaded shirt straps have been sewn on. *Denver Art Museum*

BELOW Calfskin robe painted with the "border and box" design, circa 1880. Geometric designs such as this, were worn chiefly by women and girls. *Norman Paulson, North Dakota State Historical Society*

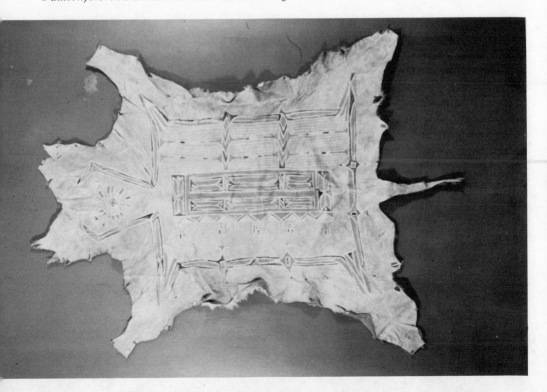

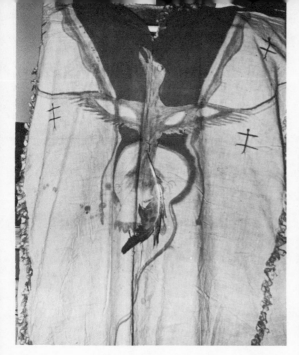

ABOVE LEFT Sioux Ghost Dance shirt (front). *Denver Art Museum*

ABOVE RIGHT Sioux Ghost Dance dress. Designs painted with house paint on tenting cloth which is lightweight and more readily cut and worn than ship's canvas. This specimen was collected in 1890 by Reese Kincaide, trader, Colony, Oklahoma, and purchased from him by the late Frederic H. Douglas, former curator of Native Arts, Denver Art Museum. *Denver Art Museum*

BELOW Ghost Dance at Traders Store, Fort Sill. Comanches, Cheyennes, and Arapahos. *U.S. Army Field Artillery and Fort Sill Museum*

her to me.' Who are you? You look like one of our own people. Are you Cheyenne?''

''I am Cheyenne,'' the young man proudly said. ''I have been a Cheyenne as long as there have been Cheyennes.''

''You are too young,'' the chief protested. ''You could not have lived that long.''

''I am as young as I am old,'' said the suitor, ''but I will make your daughter a good husband.''

''We will ask her,'' the chief said, and sent for the girl.

When she saw the handsome, well-dressed young man, with two fine bay horses, the girl hung her head shyly, and thought he would make a very good husband. So she agreed, and they were married.

After a while, the husband said, ''There is one thing that you must never do. Never turn your back on me.''

''Why not?'' asked the young wife, who was curious, like most women.

''Because I tell you not to. Something bad will happen if you do,'' her husband told her.

When they had been married about a year, a son was born. The father was very pleased and happy, and as soon as the little boy could sit up straight, the man began putting his son on the saddle behind him and teaching him to ride.

''Don't do that,'' the mother protested. ''He's too little to start riding yet.''

''I know more about this than you do,'' her husband growled.

''Maybe you know more about riding, but not about babies,'' she exclaimed, and snatched the boy down and began to run away with him.

''I told you never to turn your back on me!'' her husband howled. He got down off his horse and started chasing her.

The woman ran and ran, and she heard him pounding behind her. Once she turned her head and looked back. There was a great grizzly bear chasing her, not a man at all.

''I'll catch you and eat both of you,'' he threatened.

The woman was running to the east, and all of a sudden she saw a little mound of earth ahead of her. It was not much, but it was better than nothing. She ran to its top.

''Oh, Maheo, Above Person,'' she wept, ''help me. Help me.''

Maheo looked down and saw her and took pity on her. The mound of earth began to grow up into the air, carrying the woman and the little boy with it. When the bear got there, and saw what was happening, he was very angry.

"I'll get you yet!" he roared, and began clawing at the side of the mound, trying to get a foothold so he could climb it. But the mound kept on growing until it turned into a great sandstone butte, and the bear was left raging at the bottom. That night Maheo sent the girl's father to get her and take her home where she and her child would be safe.

Today, if you go to Bear Butte, you can still see the claw marks the bear made when he tried to climb it, and if the light is right, you can see the moccasin tracks of the woman and the little boy at the bottom. It is one place in the old Cheyenne country where women can go to look for power.

Jessie American Horse, Northern Cheyenne, Lame Deer, Montana

The Traders from Mexico

KIOWA

Trade goods played a much more important part in Indian life than is generally realized. Traders' supply lists are long and detailed. Many of them read like the inventories of general stores, going far beyond the usual trade beads, knives, and whiskey.

The earliest trade goods in the southern Plains came from Mexico. Since the last of the sixteenth century, Mexican trade had long passed back and forth between Camarugo, Chihuahua, Durango, and other northern Mexican cities to El Paso, Santa Fe, and Taos. It was only natural, after horses came into general use, that the Plains Indians should make journeys westward, not only to procure more horses but also to trade with the townsmen of the Pueblos. In time, great trading fairs were established at Taos and Tucumcari, New Mexico, among other places. It was to these centers of trade that the Mexicans made annual expeditions. In time, they enlarged their packs, and traveled eastward across the Staked Plains of the Texas Panhandle, where the Comanches had marked the water holes with yucca stalks, to trade with the tribes living beyond.

The generic name for the Mexican traders was Comancheros, but their commerce was not confined to any one tribe. They visited the Comanche, the Kiowa, the Cheyenne, and Arapaho, and some went as far east as the Kansa, Osage, and Ponca. They brought cloth, usually cotton; some beads; rum or brandy (well watered down); knives, and

111

some guns and ammunition. Often they also brought raw sugar, and other foods the Plains Indians did not know before.

The Comancheros have been largely overlooked because their numbers were relatively few, and the great bulk of trade came to the Plains from French Louisiana and St. Louis. Much more attention has been devoted to the wars and raids between the Plains Indians and the Texans than to the traders. It has sometimes been assumed that the Plains tribes categorically disliked and warred on all traders, but that was not the case. Traders from Durango and Chihuahua came up the Rio Grande to Santa Fe, and then southeast into the Plains. Traders were always welcome, and, while wagon trains from the east were frequently set upon and looted, the men from the west with the mules were relatively immune from assault.

The story that follows was told by a woman who not only remembered the Comancheros, but remembered them as the first white men she ever saw. She was born in the mid-1800s, and of course there had been white men on the Plains for more than a century before that time, but few of them had traveled into the Kiowa country.

At first, the story was a personal folktale. As the years passed it was altered in telling. The story is now a part of Kiowa folklore.

◦━━━━◦ ◦━━━━◦

The family was very poor. There was the mother, and two little girls, for their father had been killed in fighting, and there was no man to take care of them. Their father had no brothers to marry their mother, and their aunt's husband already had two wives. He helped them all he could, but he had to take care of his own family first.

Because the mother was thrifty, and dried and saved every bit of food she could get her hands on, and because she would make painted robes and moccasins for other people in exchange for meat, they were never actually hungry. The little girls were taught to dig prairie potatoes and wild turnips; to gather all the edible berries: wild currants, chokecherries, sand plums, and grapes, and to dry them as each came in season. In the fall they gathered walnuts, pecans, and hickory nuts, and in the evenings they cracked and shelled them, and stored them in rawhide cases the mother had made.

When she had time, the mother painted her rawhide storage cases and the little girls' dresses. She even made a painted robe for Older

Sister, but she would not let the girl wear it except at Sun Dance time, when everybody put on their best clothes. The rest of the time it was packed away with wild sage and the balm that is still called Indian perfume, and that keeps everything fresh and sweet-smelling.

One day some of the boys, who had been out herding horses, came running back into camp.

"Strangers are coming!" they shouted. "Strangers are coming from the west!"

"Are they armed?" asked the peace chief.

"We don't know," said one of the boys. "But they are driving mules with great packs on their backs, not on poles behind them."

"They must be Mexicans," remarked the peace chief. "If so, they have come to trade."

"What should we do?" Older Sister's mother asked.

"Wait and see," answered the peace chief. "If they are not coming to fight, but to trade, see what they have that you want."

The loaded mules traveled slowly, and it was from middle of the morning until noon before the strangers came into camp. They knew some sign language, because they held up their empty hands, palms out, to show that they came in peace. Then they made the sign for "Mexican," curving their fingers over their upper lips.

The peace chief signed with the first two fingers of his right hand, held close together and pushing toward the Mexicans to show that they were going along together. Then he rubbed his hand across his stomach, to show that there was food for the visitors if they were hungry. The Mexicans smiled and nodded, and put their own fingers inside their mouths to show that they were ready to eat. Then they followed the peace chief to the tipi where his wives had a fire started and buffalo ribs were roasting over it.

Older Sister and Younger Sister stood and watched. After all the men had eaten and smoked, the women came forward. In their turn they ate, and then gave the rest of the food to the children. When everybody was full, the Mexicans unloaded their packs. They brought out things the children had never seen before, although the older people seemed to know what they were. There was cloth, softer even than fawn skin, and in a great many different colors. Some of it had designs on it—small little designs, like flowers. It was pretty.

Then the Mexicans brought out knives; some of them great, long double-edged for the men, and some smaller, but sharp, for the women to use. They had the feathers of some strange birds, very bright-colored, and some shiny things made of metal, but not the same metals as the knives. There were earrings and bracelets and rings, and a small pile of solid metal disks that some of the Kiowa men must have known about, because they looked at them longer and more carefully than at anything else.

And then the Mexicans unloaded a small round thing, like a kettle, but made of wood with metal bands around it and a sealed-tight lid, and the Kiowa men began to laugh. The Mexican chief took out a cup, made of still another kind of shiny metal, and turned a handle on the side of the bucket. Colored water ran into the cup, and the Mexican offered it to the peace chief. He drank it all right down, and then he choked and sputtered, and then he turned to his wives. "Run and get some things if you want to trade," he ordered, and some of the other men did the same thing.

Older Sister and Younger Sister stood and watched. They wondered if the Mexicans had anything for children. The things they had seen so far, even the colored water, were all for grownups. And the men wouldn't let their wives have even a taste of that.

One of the younger Mexicans went to his mule, and began unfastening its pack. He took out lumps of brown hard stuff, and with the handle of his knife cracked off two pieces. He smiled at the children and handed them each one. They stood and looked at it and the Mexican broke off another piece and put it in his mouth. Then they understood. This was something for children to eat. When they tasted it, it was sweeter than anything they had ever eaten before.

"Gusto?" asked the Mexican. That must be the name of the stuff.

"Gusto," they assured him, but then they were suddenly puzzled. Everybody else was trading with the Mexicans, but they had nothing of their own to trade. The tipi and everything in it belonged to their mother. Then Older Sister remembered. She had her robe—her painted robe!

Older Sister slipped out of the crowd and went back to the tipi by herself. She opened the painted case where the robe was kept, and took it out, with her hands shaking a little. But it was the only thing she had of her own that she could trade, and it was beautiful. Quickly, before she could change her mind, she went back to the crowd and found the young Mexican.

He was still chipping pieces of the sweet stuff and giving it to the children. Some of them were even holding out their hands for more, and didn't seem to think about trading. But Older Sister wanted to do what was right. She stood in front of the man, and held out the robe to him.

He looked down at her, standing there, a little girl about seven, in an old smoked buckskin dress made from one of her mother's, and suddenly, he put out his hand and stroked her hair. Then he took the robe, and held it up to see it. And then he folded it carefully, painted side in, and handed it back to her.

"No," said the young Mexican man, "No, Niña." And he gave her another piece of the sweet stuff, and another one to Younger Sister.

* * *

Older Sister, Kiowa
A longer version of this story, told by another informant, appears in The Ten Grandmothers *by Alice Marriott, number twenty-sixth in the Civilization of the American Indian Series, University of Oklahoma Press, Norman, Oklahoma, 1945.*

The Woman General

OSAGE

By 1800, the Plains Indians were in a state of turmoil. Indians were being removed from the eastern states, or removing themselves, displacing the Osage and Quapaw, among other groups. These formerly waterborne peoples became horseback Indians, and raided westward, going so far as to attack a Kiowa camp in the Wichita Mountains in 1835.

St. Louis had become a city; New Orleans had been one for over a century. Traffic up and down the Mississippi, at first on roped or poled keelboats and barges, later by steamboats trailing the barges, steadily increased between the two once-French cities. Emigrants, German farmers particularly, spread out from the centers and began farms to supply the cities' needs. The Austins were colonizing Texas; John Law and his Scotts colony had moved northward from Louisiana into Arkansas, and the Mississippi bubble had burst, scattering colonists westward. It was clear to everyone that the white men were here to stay.

It was a time of great temptation. By raiding white settlements and isolated farms and ranches, the Plains Indians could drive off horses and mules, butcher cattle when they were short of buffalo or venison; and sometimes capture women and children. The women could be put to work; the children adopted by an Indian family, usually to replace a child who had died. Stories of captives are numerous; sometimes the

116

captive actually came from another tribe, sometimes it was a frontier white child. Most of the latter seem to have adapted readily to Indian life.

Such a child was Maria James, who was found wandering alone in eastern Arkansas about 1830 by the Osages, who adopted her, and she grew up among them.

The little girl had wandered away from the farmyard into the woods. She was not looking for anything in particular. She found a wild grapevine and swung herself back and forth on its great rope for a while, then went on. She had no brothers or sisters to play with and sometimes she was lonely.

She heard voices ahead of her, and walked toward them. Soon she saw people moving through the woods, gathering the wild grapes. There were women and children, a small group of them. She knew there were other settlers in these woods, but these did not look like anyone she had ever seen. Their language was strange, too. They must be Indians.

Her mother had warned her that the Indians stole white children, and if she ever saw any, she must go home at once. But then one of the women turned and saw her, and smiled—a kind smile. Maria stood hesitating, and the woman held out a bunch of grapes. She even ate one, to show that they were safe. Maria took the bunch and ate the rest of it. She drifted with the group, and before she realized it, they had come into a cluster of mat-covered houses, all arranged to face east. She followed the woman who had given her the grapes, and who stooped and entered one of the lodges. Maria followed her inside.

The woman turned and saw her, a fair-haired little girl in an old dress, barefoot, because it was not yet time for her father to go down to the river landing and trade for shoes. "You—name?" the woman asked carefully in broken English.

"Maria James."

"Where you live?"

That startled Maria. She had lost all sense of time and direction, trailing through the woods. She shook her head.

"You stay here?"

Maria stood and thought. She was not sure where home was, or how to get there. Her mother would surely whip her if she went home now, but if she stayed where she was perhaps her parents would come looking for her. She had been away in the woods all day, and the kettle of soup steaming over the fire in the middle of the lodge smelled good. She nodded.

"I stay."

She stayed the rest of her life. The family she had adopted were good to her; they made her clothes, from buckskin and from trade cloth. She wore the soft-soled two-piece Osage moccasins. She learned to plait mats and sashes, and to sew the big cattail mats to cover the lodge, using twisted nettle cord and a bone needle. She learned the things an Osage woman was supposed to know and do, but sometimes she was bored.

It was at such a time, when she felt idle and dull, that she saw the boys playing with their bows and arrows, and asked to borrow a bow. The boys laughed at her.

"Girls don't shoot," they said.

"I'm going to," Maria answered.

"You can't. We won't let you," the boys told her.

Maria went home. She told her adopted father what she wanted, and although he too laughed at her, he showed her how to make a bow and arrows. "You won't play with them long," he assured her.

To everybody's surprise but her own, Maria did. She watched every step of the bow making. She saw her Osage father take a straight, seasoned length of bois d'arc from the rafters of the house, build a fire outside, and warm the wood slowly over it, turning it evenly in his hands when he did so. She watched while he began slowly and evenly to bend the wood into a curve. He measured it against her and made it long enough for her to grow into it. When the curve fitted her, he stopped.

"Now you can make your own bowstring," he directed her.

Maria went to her own supply of sinew. She had been learning to make moccasins, and there was a good-sized slab of the sinew left. She split it with the point of her knife, not as finely as she would for moccasins, and when she had a pile, she began twisting it into a cord over her thigh, as she had been taught to twist nettle fiber. When she had to join another piece of sinew to her twist, she chewed each end until they were thoroughly moist and would hold together. She went on twisting until her skin was raw and sore, but when she finished she had a cord half again as long as the bow.

"Now let it dry overnight," her Osage father told her.

In the morning he showed her how to wrap the cord around one end of the bow, until it was secure. Then he showed her how to loop the other end, slip it over the head of the bow, and tighten it with a piece of bone. When it was as tight as she could make it, he lent her an arrow.

"See if you can pull it," he said.

It was a hard pull, and loosing the arrow was even harder, but Maria learned. She learned how to make her own arrows, attaching to them four straight splits of hawk quill. And she learned how to hunt.

The first time she brought down a deer, and brought it home, her Osage mother was horrified. "You act like a boy," she said. "Why you're almost grown up enough to be married. You ought to be ashamed of yourself."

"Boys have more fun than girls," Maria protested.

"If you want to act like a boy," her mother said, "then do what a boy would do. Take your first game, and give it to Old Lady Walking Around. She's poor and alone and needs the meat."

When Old Lady Walking Around saw Maria coming with the deer, she began to laugh. "What do you think you're doing?" she asked. "Girls don't shoot deer."

"I shot this one and I want you to have it," Maria said proudly. And she laid the deer on the ground before Old Lady Walking Around. "You are my mother's friend, and she told me to bring it to you."

"Then I thank you, and her," replied Old Lady Walking Around. "I will dry some of it for her."

From that time on, Maria was accepted as a tomboy. She hunted and rode with the men and boys, although she always dressed like a girl, and wore her long fair hair loose over her shoulders as all the women did. Sometimes the boys would tease her about that, and tell her she ought to have her head shaved except for a crest on top, as the Osage men did, but Maria refused to do that.

When she was about fourteen, and the boys her own age were going on a war party, Maria wanted to go, too.

"You can't do that," her father said, sternly. "No decent woman would go with a war party—only one who was eloping with her lover and wanted to get away from her husband. People will talk about you. They'll laugh at you."

"I'm going," Maria declared, and she went.

She took her part in the war party as a man. There was usually a boy assigned to war parties to cook and work for the men, but Maria refused to do that kind of work. She still dressed like a woman, but she could fight like a man, and fight well, too. The men respected her.

From time to time, after that, word would get back to St. Louis, from some fur trader or trapper, about a fair young woman who rode out with the Osage war and hunting parties. Nobody knew who she was, but she was seen occasionally. Not until a priest visited the camp was her identity known. By that time she could barely speak English. But she remembered her name.

"Come home," the priest suggested. "You should go back to your own people."

"These are my own people," Maria declared.

"But you are a white woman, my child. You should marry a white man, and have children."

"I don't know any white men except the traders and trappers," said Maria, "and I don't want one of them. They smell bad."

Eventually the priest gave up urging Maria to change her way of life. Maria thought about what he had said, though, and when her Indian father called her and said he wanted to speak seriously to her, she listened.

"Rising Star has asked for you," announced her father. "He is a good man, a few years older than you are, and will make you a good husband."

"I'll talk to him," Maria promised.

"And listen to him, too," her father warned.

Maria sat and thought about what her adopted father had said. She was a tomboy, and as strong as any man, but perhaps there were other things in life for a woman to do. She looked around the village. None of the women rode on war parties, but they seemed happy and contented; their faces and their voices showed peace realized and achieved. It could be that part of Maria's life was incomplete.

When Rising Star came to the lodge that evening, to speak to her father again, Maria was ready to listen to him. She sat quietly on her mat, with her legs folded under her, to the right, woman-fashion. It was stiff and uncomfortable for her to sit this way—she was used to sitting like a man, with her legs straight out—but it was part of that woman's life she had decided to learn. With her head down, she listened to her father tell her of the gifts she would receive from Rising Star's family, and of the horses he would give them in return.

"You will give away a great deal in my honor," she finally said.

"You mean a lot to both of us," her father assured her.

"If we marry, you can't always go out with the war parties," Rising Star said. "You can go hunting, but not fighting. Besides, if we have children, you won't be able to."

"No," Maria answered. "That would be dangerous for the child."

"That's right," Rising Star agreed. "You don't want to put the child in danger, even if you don't care about yourself."

She married Rising Star, and in time they had four children. Maria was no tomboy, now. Usually she did a woman's work in the village, but sometimes she went hunting, and brought in her own meat.

The men she had ridden with did not forget her. Before each raid, they consulted her, and she told them what she thought would be the best way to approach an Indian tribal settlement or a white farmstead. Usually they followed her advice, and were glad she had given it. Even when she was an old, old woman, with grandchildren around her, the men came to her for advice.

By this time she was well known enough to be called by the whites "the Woman General." They were afraid of her good planning mind. When she died, she was buried like a man, and they piled a mound of earth over her body.

From Osage records; teller unknown

The Woman Left on the Prairie

COMANCHE

Maria James was fortunate in her voluntary captivity, but not all women fared so well. The Comanches were always noted for their aggressiveness, and for their cruelty.

A story persists that there was a "Comanche West Point" somewhere in the Sierra Madres, in the state of Chihuahua, Mexico, and that young warriors were sent there for training. It has even been hinted that the commandant of this military installation was a woman, but that hardly seems likely. Certainly most Comanche women must have been kept busy by ordinary household chores. The story that follows shows the other side of Maria James's coin.

The Comanche War Party had been raiding for horses in Mexico, and were driving the herd they had captured north, to cross the Red River. They were about halfway to the river when they found the hacienda. It stood in a grove of trees, not far from a running stream. The big adobe house had two stories. The Comanches had never seen anything like it, and they stopped to look. There was fruit on some of the trees, and since they had eaten nothing much but dried meat and mesquite meal for months, the men helped themselves to the sweet plums and apricots.

Strangely, there seemed to be no one about. It was a hot afternoon and the stillness was broken only by the sounds of the bees in their hives behind the house, and the creaking of a windmill, from whose pump water was flowing into a tank.

The heavy wooden door was closed. "Let's go inside and see what these people have," the leader of the war party suggested. "Maybe there are other things to eat in there." He pushed on the door and it rolled back on the posts set into the door sill and lintel, which served as hinges. The silence continued.

There was a hall before them, and beyond that an open garden where flowers were growing. On the other side of the garden was another room, with a fire burning in a square adobe box that was faced with painted, shiny squares. There was a table, and food stood on it. They helped themselves to the meat and flat breads, and stood there eating and looking around them.

They heard a scream, and turned to see a woman standing in the doorway. Her black hair streamed down over her white blouse and red skirt. She wore shoes with props under them that lifted her heels up in the air, not letting them stay flat, like moccasins. Her skin was light, and her hands soft.

"Madre de Dios!" she cried again, and turned, and ran across the garden, down the hall, and out to the front of the house. There was a metal bell on a platform there, and the woman reached for the hammer that lay beside it, and lifted her arm to pound metal on metal.

The war chief reached her in time to grab her arm and pull the hammer away. He crushed his other hand over her mouth, and held her, with her back to him while she stiffened in his arms. Then, while he still gripped her, the fight went out of her and she was limp, like a hurt bird.

The chief tore off a piece of her skirt and tied her mouth with it. Then he set her on his horse in front of him, still holding her with one hand while the other rose and fell with his quirt pounding his horse. He gripped and guided the barebacked horse with his knees. The whole party galloped away as fast as they could push the horse herd along. Some of the chief's blows fell on the woman instead of the horse, and once she cried out in pain when the rawhide cut her arm, but most of the time she was as silent as she was helpless.

Not until nightfall did they stop. By then the party was out on the open prarie. The men tied the woman and laid her on the ground while they ate.

"What shall we do with her?" one man asked when they finished.

"She's pretty," said the chief. "I'll take her home with me. I have only two wives, and I can afford another."

"That's not fair," another man objected. "We all took her, and she should belong to all of us."

"No," protested the chief. "I took her. I picked her up and rode with her all day. She belongs to me."

"She belongs to everyone," another man declared. "We will all have her, here and now."

And so they did, each man raping the woman in turn, until her cries of pain died away to little whimpering sounds.

"Now you can take her," the others said to the chief.

"No," the chief answered. "A woman marries if she is pure. No Comanche wants a woman that any man can take. Leave her here."

And in the morning they rode away and left her, lying on the prairie.

Told by Ira Mae Wahnee, Comanche

Enemies

PAWNEE

*Elsewhere, we have spoken of the Pawnees as "everybody's enemies,"
and so, in a sense they were. But they also were capable of enmity
toward each other, as the story that follows shows.*

*It must date back, when the Pawnees had acquired horses, but were
still living in earth lodges. The names of the characters have been lost,
and the story has been told and retold so often that it has truly taken
on the character of a legend, and has given rise to a saying among
other Indians, "Getting even like a Pawnee." The story must truly be
regarded as a legend, for although it concerns real people, they are
prototypes.*

Like many Pawnee stories, it begins:

Once upon a time, there were two cousins who were always quarreling. We call them Gray Fox and Black Bear, but of course those
weren't their real names, because we don't usually speak the names of
the people who are gone.

But they were always quarreling. If Gray Fox killed a buffalo,
Black Bear wanted the hide and the hump, which is the best meat. If
Black Bear killed two wild turkeys, Gray Fox wanted the bigger one.
It was like that all the time. They were cousins, so they had to share
with each other.

So they went on a war party. The leader didn't want to take both of them, but they both bragged so much that finally he gave in.

"I can kill twenty enemies," Gray Fox boasted.

"Anybody can kill enemies," Black Bear retorted, "but I can ride up to forty and touch them with my bare hand."

"We'll see which of you is the better man," said the leader. "The Sioux will show us soon enough."

They started out, riding to the north and west, where the Sioux live, and it was a long way. They crossed rivers, and they rode among the trees along the river banks, and they rode through the sand hills of western Nebraska. They were used to rivers, and those didn't bother them. They just threw some tobacco in, in case of water monsters, and went on. Then they came to the sand hills and that was different.

"How can we keep together going up and down these soft hills?" Gray Fox asked the leader.

"Just ride zigzag up and down the hills," the leader ordered.

Gray Fox started out, riding zigzag in one direction and Black Bear started out going the opposite way. The war party went straight ahead, but pretty soon they realized two of their members were missing. Everybody had to turn back and hunt for Gray Fox and Black Bear, and it took all day.

"Stupid!" said the leader.

"He's stupid," said Gray Fox pointing with his chin at Black Bear. "I knew he was going the wrong way all the time. He's always getting lost. That's the kind of man he is."

"*I* was going right." Black Bear protested. "He's the one that's always getting mixed up."

"I want you both to ride right beside me from now on," the leader ordered. "That way, if we get lost we'll all get lost together."

Pretty soon they found horse tracks, and they knew the Sioux were ahead of them. Then the country opened out to the high plains, and they could see a village beside a river. The marks of the women's horse drags were very plain now, on the dry earth. The Sioux had just finished setting up camp and the women were getting the cooking fires started.

"Let's charge them!" cried Gray Fox.

"Be quiet," the leader ordered. "Wait until night, and then we can get them."

"I'm hungry," said Black Bear. "Let's start a cooking fire ourselves, and have some meat."

"Cooking fire!" said everybody else, "Why they can see the smoke as far as we can see theirs."

So they waited until it was dark and the Sioux camp had settled down. They had some dried meat with them, and they leaned their teeth into that, and drank some water from a little creek, and went on waiting. When everything below was still, they started towards the Sioux camp.

But the Sioux had suspected something, and they had their scouts out. The Pawnees didn't get a chance to kill or touch any of the Sioux, but they did get away with a horse apiece. The Sioux didn't even bother to come after them. They had plenty of horses, and the ones the Pawnees got weren't very good anyway.

Well, after the war party got home, Gray Fox and Black Bear fell in love. They both fell in love with the same girl. Her father was the chief of the village, and the girl was very beautiful. But she wasn't in love with Gray Fox or Black Bear, but with the chief of the war party, so she married him.

It went on and on that way, the two cousins always arguing about something, and each of them trying to show off how much better he was than the other. People got tired of their foolishness, and told them so. Or, worse, they didn't even notice them. That made Gray Fox and Black Bear madder than anything else.

Finally, Gray Fox decided to settle it. He got his best horse—he had several by that time—and he took a sweat bath, and plucked out every hair on his head except his crest with a pair of sharp mussel shells he got from the creek. He painted his face with yellow earth with black charcoal stripes across it, because those were his clan colors, and he put on his best leggings and moccasins and breechclout.

He braided colored cloth into his horse's mane and tail, and he smoothed it all down with a porcupine tail. By the time Gray Fox had finished, he and his horse looked very fine indeed.

Then Gray Fox got on the horse and rode over to Black Bear's lodge.

"Come out, cousin," he called.

Black Bear climbed up the ladder through the smoke hole in the roof of the lodge, and stood there, looking down at Gray Fox.

"Here, cousin," Gray Fox said, "I have a present for you. Come here." Black Bear came down the side of the lodge and stood there, still looking at Gray Fox and still not saying anything.

Gray Fox got down off his horse. He took off his leggings and breechclout and moccasins and laid them across the horse's back. He took the lines and handed the horse to Black Bear.

"There, cousin," Gray Fox said, and walked back across the village with nothing on but his paint. That way he got even. He made everybody laugh at Black Bear because Gray Fox had shown to all just how greedy Black Bear was.

Dolly Moore, Pawnee

The Winter the Stars Fell– 1833-1834

KIOWA

The great meteor shower of the nineteenth century can be regarded as the true beginning of formally recorded history on the Plains. This starfall was visible all over North America; even Nigh's Weekly Register, *a newsletter published in London, recorded it.*

There had been single and even clustered falling stars before, but never a time when, for night after night, it seemed that all Heaven was descending on the earth. Then, abruptly, the fall stopped, and nothing like it has ever been seen again.

A few years later there was an eclipse of the sun over the southern Plains, and terror spread among the tribes again. Both events were recorded in the Kiowa "calendars," or year counts, and could be clearly described a hundred years later.

In 1892, when James Mooney recorded the first year count to come to his attention, the Kiowas were thought to be the only Plains tribe to keep year counts and to have a clear, historical sense of the passage of time. Later a number of records came to light among the various northern Siouan groups, and it has been said that both Cheyenne and Arapaho kept yearly records, although these have been lost or destroyed.

The records were made, uniformly, by a series of drawings which began in the middle of a buckskin and spiraled outwards. The main event of each winter and each summer was drawn, with Sun Dance

Lodge above the drawings for summer and a black bar or a leafless tree above the winter drawings.

It was Kiowa custom, during the summer Sun Dance, for the older men of all bands to gather in council and discuss the preceding season's events. The event chosen for summer and the event chosen for winter as most important were then added to the record. Sometimes these events were of recognizable importance, like the first dragoon expedition across the Plains, smallpox epidemics, or battles with other tribes. Sometimes the events were more personal: a man and woman eloped, a man was scalped by the Utes, a person who later became important was born. One winter was so cold that the Horses Ate the Ashes of the Camp Fires.

Here, then, is the story of the meteor shower and the eclipse, as recorded and told in 1934, by the last of the official Kiowa record keepers, then in his nineties.

You can see in this picture that there are many, many stars. I was not born then, but my mother was a young woman growing up, and she saw the stars fall out of the sky, and never forgot it. She used to tell us about it.

The winter camp was in the Big Bend of the Washita River that year. We were the Bull Elk band, and while we used to go there later, in summer, when it was Sun Dance time and safe, we never made a winter camp again in that place.

It was an open winter. No big snows, just frost on the ground in the mornings. There were even some leaves still hanging on the cottonwood trees, and of course the scrub oaks were covered with dry leaves that wouldn't fall till next spring.

It was a safe camp. There was water on three sides of the bend, and we put up brush windbreaks around the tipis. The children played and helped with herding the horses, and the women cooked and made moccasins and all kinds of clothes. Some of the men were always going hunting. We had plenty to eat, in those old days. Not like the starving times that came afterward.

One evening a man went out of his wife's tipi. Maybe he had a reason —maybe he just wanted to look around—I don't know. Anyway, all at once he let out a great shout, ''The stars are falling! The whole sky is falling!''

The people came running out of their tipis, all excited and shouting: "What is happening? What do you mean? Is the world coming to an end?" Nobody knew what to say or do.

There were two men in camp who were guardians of two of those Grandmother medicine power bundles that protect all the Kiowas. They ran to their wives' tipis and brought out the bundles. Everybody prayed to them, but the stars just kept on falling. They fell and fell, every night, for many nights. It didn't seem as if there could be any stars left in the sky at all. Then all of a sudden it was spring, and the stars stopped falling.

As I told you, I do not know these things myself, but my mother was there, and she saw, and told me. In the summer, when the old men came together to talk about what had happened, and make a picture of something important, they put down the falling stars. Then they looked back and saw that two years before a war party had held up a wagon train, going west, on the Arkansas River, in what you call Kansas. They killed the teamsters and took things out of the wagons. Some of the bags were full of silver money. The Kiowas didn't know what to do with money, and some of them threw theirs away because it was heavy, but some of the others brought theirs back, and when the Mexican traders came, they swapped it to them.

So then the old men decided that the Americans punished them for that raid by making the stars fall. Long, long afterward, they found out the Americans hadn't made the stars fall, and were just as frightened as the Kiowas when they saw them.

The next summer, or maybe it was the one after that, there was a big camp out at End of the Mountains, west of the Wichita Mountains. They were getting ready for the Sun Dance, so people were coming in and coming in.

And then, right at noon, when people were starting to eat dinner, it began to get dark. It got darker and darker—just like midnight. All the people were frightened again.

"The sun is dying!" they yelled. "A snake has come up from under the world and is swallowing the sun! What shall we do? What shall we do?"

There was one very strong medicine man in camp. His power was the bobcat, and that's the strongest power there is. He came out, all painted up as well as he could in the darkness, and began to shake his rattle and dance and sing, screaming like a bobcat, as if he were curing a sick person.

Pretty soon there was a little rim of light, like the edge of a finger-nail, up in the sky. The medicine man danced and sang harder and harder, and the light grew and grew, until the whole sun came out in the sky and the world was alive again. The birds came out of their nests and began to sing; the young men and women laughed, and the mothers went back to getting dinner.

Then all the people honored that medicine man and gave him pres-ents. They didn't know what made the sun go away, but they did know who brought it back so they could have the Sun Dance that year, as they always did.

Told to Alice Marriott by "Kiowa George" Poolaw; translated by Justin Poolaw I, Kiowa

Tipi Shaking

MESCALERO APACHE

The Mescalero Apache, of southeastern New Mexico, are a marginal Plains tribe, in the same sense that the Osage are, but on the west, rather than on the east. The Mescalero were buffalo hunters, who came down from the mountains near present Ruidoso, New Mexico, seasonally onto the Plains surrounding what is now Roswell.

Mescalero buffalo hunting was essentially Plains hunting, with chosen men (not societies) to keep order and act as game wardens and camp police. In pre-Conquest times the Mescalero undoubtedly hunted by driving the buffalo over a cliff into a canyon, for bone piles that evidence such hunting have been found in the area. Later, the Mescalero hunted on horseback, or, preferably, on muleback. The mules made better meat than horses in starving times, all Apaches said. Burros, which they kept for mule breeding and as pack animals, made the best meat of all, if there were no game.

The country in that remote part of the world is eerie. The mountains rise high and black, covered with Ponderosa pines, or red and sheer, menacing walls of basalt. The great White Sands desert, the world's first atomic proving ground, lies beneath the red stone pipes of the Organ Mountains. Its animal life is colorless—transparent crickets and scorpions run in the sand and desert rats and mice are protectively white. Roads seem to run downhill, until you notice an automobile's motor heating dangerously, and looking back, realize that you have been driving uphill.

That is the west barrier of the Mescalero country. To the east, near Roswell, at the right time of year and in the right light, stretch miles of water—a mirage that retreats to the eastern horizon, very slowly, as one approaches it. Northward runs the Jornada de Muerto (Dead Man's Road), from El Paso to Santa Fe, paralleling the Rio Grande, but the Mescaleros do not travel in that direction. Their road is east or west, depending on the season.

Like their Athabascan-speaking brothers, from north to south, from the Arctic Circle to the Sierra Madres of northern Mexico, the Mescaleros do not live in true tipis, but in cone-shaped brush shelters. These are sometimes called tipis, especially when the speaker is addressing a non-Indian, but it would be more accurate to refer to them as wickiups. Their support poles protrude from a smoke hole in the roof, tipi-fashion, however, and as the teller of the following story said, "Anything that can happen in a wickiup could happen in a tipi, too."

Roof shaking, or pole shaking, is also characteristically Athabascan. Perhaps it developed from the igloo seances of the Eskimo neighbors of the most northern Athabascan groups. It has been adopted, in a somewhat diluted form, by the Kiowa neighbors of the Athabascans.

To prophesy through the hoot of an owl implies a man of great magical powers and supreme confidence in them. The Mescaleros share the general North American Indian dread of owls and bears, and do not trifle with such forces. As far as can be determined, this is a very old legend, probably going back to pre-white times.

<hr/>

The Mescaleros were getting ready to go hunting and were camped by the big spring east of the mountains. They had brought their poles with them, and, instead of underbrush, covered them with upright cattail stalks, which the women waded into the big spring to pull.

It was a pretty big camp—maybe twenty wickiups. The Mescaleros did not make big camps like the Kiowas and Comanches. They stayed more in family groups. Then the older people could keep an eye on the younger ones, and see that they didn't get into trouble. It would be bad if a clan brother and sister fell in love with each other.

Of course the younger people didn't like being watched all the time. They knew what the danger was—they might have a baby that was crippled or deformed some way, or maybe even twins. If that happened, one would have to be killed, to put one soul together in one body. But still the young people didn't like being watched all the time.

There was one young couple especially that didn't like it. The boy was a captive, who had been taken in Mexico when he was little. He wasn't a Mescalero at all, but a Yaqui. Nobody knew what his clan was, or even if the Yaquis had clans, but he had been adopted by a Mescalero family, so he belonged to the same clan as the girl.

The girl's mother watched her for four days, and then she said,"Whenever you go for water, that boy goes a little later. Do you talk to him?"

"Sometimes," the girl said, bowing her head so her long hair fell over her face.

"Don't you know that you mustn't? He's your brother. We had the Woman-Making Dance for you two summers ago, and you should be getting married, but let your father and me choose a husband for you. Don't ever think about your brother that way."

"All right," said the girl, but she didn't say exactly what was all right, or if she would obey or disobey.

The next day, when the girl was coming back from the spring with her pitch-covered basket canteen full of water slung on her back by a line of buckskin across her forehead and over her shoulders, she met the Yaqui boy.

"Hello," he said.

"My mother told me not to talk to you," the girl replied. "We are brother and sister, and we must never speak until one of us is married."

"I know that rule," the boy said, "but it's different for us. We aren't brother and sister; I'm from another tribe."

"I am a woman, and I mustn't speak to you," the girl insisted. "My mother said so."

"Then you aren't a woman," the boy scolded. "You're a baby. You won't do anything but what your mother tells you to. Did you promise not to speak to me?"

"No," the girl whispered.

"Then come away with me," he said. "We can go back into the mountains and hide."

"I'm afraid," the girl said, and she began to cry.

"I'll take care of you," the boy insisted. "You'll be safe."

"If my father finds us he'll beat me. He might even kill me. And I know he would kill you."

"He won't find us. We'll go and find my own people. It's a long way, but we can find them, I know."

So with nothing but her knife and the basket canteen of water on her back, she went with him.

When the girl didn't come back, her mother began to worry. The sun was in mid-sky, and her daughter had left the wickiup in early morning. The mother took her own canteen and went to the spring, following the tracks of the girl's moccasins. The tracks stopped at the spring, because when they left, the boy had brushed out all the footprints with a piece of rabbit brush, so no one could follow them.

The woman went back to camp. When her husband came in, she fed him. When he had finished eating, he looked around the wickiup.

"Where is our daughter?" the father asked.

"I don't know," the mother answered. "She hasn't come back from the spring. I followed her footprints that far, but then they disappeared."

"She's gone with that boy!" the father exclaimed, his face growing dark with anger. "I know it. He's coaxed her, and stolen her away."

"Let's go talk to his family," the mother suggested.

They got up and went out of their wickiup and went to the one where the other family lived together, the father and mother were searching for their son.

"He's gone, but not hunting," the adopted father said. "See, his bow and arrows are right here hanging from the pole over his bed."

"He's gone hunting, but not that kind of game," the girl's father replied. "My daughter is gone, too."

"What are we going to do?" both women wailed.

"We'll have to find them," said the girl's father.

"Which way would they go?" the adopted father asked.

"They would have to go west. If they went east from this place, someone would see them."

"West, northwest, southwest?" the other man demanded. "They could find places to hide in any of those directions."

"We don't know where to look!" the women wept.

There happened to be an owl prophet in the camp. He was an old man, and not very strong in his body, but his mind was clear and his power was great. That was why the people had taken him with them when they went hunting. His power would help them find the buffalo.

"Let's send for that old man," the girl's father suggested. "He can find game, and horses and mules that have strayed. Surely he can tell us where to find our children, so we can bring them back."

"That's a good idea," both mothers agreed.

By that time the news had gotten all over the camp, and people had begun to gather outside the door and listen.

"He will want a lot to find them," one of the listeners said. "He wanted four buckskins to find my horse. I know he'll want more than that to find the young people.

"We can go and ask him," the adopted father said.

The four people came out of the wickiup, and leaned a stick by the doorway to show that they would be back. They went to the old man's wickiup, where he and his wife were sitting in the afternoon sun, on the other side from the doorway.

The old man's power had told him people were coming, so when they stood before him, he asked them,

"Why do you come? What do you want?"

"Our children have gone. We want to get them back before anything bad happens."

"My power can find them, but it will want some presents."

"What does it want?"

"It wants two mules, one from each family, to find the boy. For the girl, it wants four buckskins and four storage baskets."

"We can get the buckskins right away," the girl's mother said, "but it takes a long time to make those big deep baskets."

"If you can get the mules and the buckskins by this evening, my power will go right to work, because it knows you are worried. The baskets can come later, when you get them made."

"I have one I can give now," offered the boy's adopted mother.

"That's good. My wife really needs those baskets. But if she gets one now, she can wait for the others. Now, you go and get things ready. Don't eat anything more today. Just drink a little water. That's all. And make sure the wickiup is all clean. Take everything down that is hanging from the poles, so my power can get in and out of the smoke hole easily. And light just a little fire. Tie the mules west of the wickiup, and lay the basket and the buckskins on the floor west of the fire. We will be there at sundown."

When the two families left the old man, they talked things over. Among them, the four people decided to have the ceremony in the boy's mother's wickiup. It was larger, and since that family was giving the basket, they deserved the honor. It was a great honor to have a pole-shaking ceremony held in your wickiup.

The women got everything ready, and by the time the boy's mother had lighted a small fire in the hole in the middle of the floor, everybody in camp gathered around outside. The old man and his wife came last. They went into the wickiup and sat down on the west, behind the presents, and then as many of the other people as could came in. The two fathers sat north of the old man and the two mothers sat on the south, beside his wife.

When everybody was inside who could get inside, the old man asked if they were ready. He took a little Navaho pottery drum and a ring-headed drumstick from under his blanket. Then he called for a bucket of water. Someone passed it in from the doorway, and the old man poured the water over the fire, so the whole inside of the wickiup was dark. Then he began to beat his drum and sing.

He sang four songs, and then he stopped and waited. At first nothing happened. Then, far off, in the mountains to the southwest, an owl hooted.

Again the old man sang four songs, and waited. And again the owl spoke to him, nearer and louder this time.

He sang again, and again he waited. This time, when the owl spoke, it sounded as if it were right outside the wickiup.

The fourth time the old man called his power, the tops of the poles began to shake. Then there was a great blast of hot wind, and they could hear the owl flying around inside the wickiup, over their heads. It talked to the old man and he answered it. At last the owl gave one final cry, and the poles shook again as it flew away, calling as if to tell the old man which way it had gone.

"Thank you," said the old man. "I will tell them your message." He sat very quietly until the last sound died away, and then he told the women to build up the fire. In its light they could see how tired he looked, as if he had been on a long journey and come back on foot.

"My power says," he told the people, "that your young people have gone away to the southwest to look for the Yaquis, his people. They are on the edge of the White Sands now. If you men go quickly, and start right at daylight, you can catch them. They aren't married yet. The girl doesn't want to marry him until they have seen the Yaquis.''

Then the old people got up, and took their presents, and went back to their own wickiup, walking very slowly, because using strong power does make a man tired.

In the morning the two fathers, with two of their brothers, set out. They traveled hard and fast and far, and by nightfall they came to a little camp in the open, on the edge of the White Sands, where the young couple were. Their fathers greeted them, and in the morning they all went home. Everybody was so happy they came back, and nothing had happened, that the parents forgot to beat the young people.

When the girl's mother took the fourth basket to the old man, he said to her, ''Sit down. My power has been talking to me. Because they are not really brother and sister, and because he knows where his own people live, they may marry. Nothing bad will happen to anybody, my power says.''

So the mothers made a great feast, and the two were married, and that is why the Mescaleros call the Yaquis their brothers.

James Kawaykula, Mescalero

Wolf Power

KIOWA

Timber wolves simply did not occur in the Plains area for lack of timber. Prairie wolves and coyotes are much smaller than the true timber wolf. It is hardly surprising, then, that people of the Plains tribes, on those rare occasions when they saw the great gray-black beasts, were awed by them.

The legend that follows dates from a very early time, but the events it tells of show that some of the Kiowa were, even then, established in what is still their home territory—the sweep of short grass country between the Wichita Mountains in southwestern Oklahoma and the Arkansas River, in Kansas. A similar story, from the Sioux, has been recorded by Stanley Vestal, in The Missouri, *University of Nebraska Press, Bison Series, Lincoln, Nebraska, 1964.*

The Kiowa name for the Wichita Mountains, collectively, is the same as the English: Wichita Mountains, although each low peak has its own name too: Saddle Mountain, which has kept its name in English translation; Power Mountain now known as Mount Scott, and Hiding Mountain, into which the buffalo were said to have disappeared, now known as Cement Mountain from the quarry which defaces its east side.

The Arkansas River was Say-say-paw, or Arrowhead River, for it was along the banks near its headwaters that the Kiowa found the quartz pebbles they chipped to make knives, spearheads, and arrow-

heads. It was an established practice for any war or hunting party that reached that stretch of the river to load its members with as many rough cores as the men could carry, to be worked down later at home. There were specialists in weapon making, and the finder was expected to divide his cores equally with the expert. This practice holds true today, in the "make one and keep one" expertise of fan making or rattle decorating.

The hunting party were members of the Big Shield band of Kiowas. They were camped on the Washita River when they decided to go up into the Lodge Pole Mountains (the Colorado Rockies), where the great straight pines grow, and hunt for Utes. They were always fighting with the Utes in those days.

Bird-Tied-on-His-Head was the leader. It was the fourth time he had taken a war party out. He had gone against the Jicarilla Apaches, the Navahos, and the Pueblos Who Fight (Taos). Each time he beat the enemy. Now he was going against the Utes, who were the most dangerous of all.

There were twelve of them altogether including the Buffalo Doctor, and the man who was next to Bird-Tied-on-His-Head was his brother, Buffalo Roars. They had four young boys with them to lead the extra horses and to do the herding when they stopped. The boys took turns cooking, too, when it was safe to light a fire. The rest of time they lived on dried meat and mesquite bean meal and cold water. Of course, they didn't know anything about coffee then.

The war party went northwest, out across the Staked Plains. The only Indians they were likely to see would be Comanches, who were friendly, or maybe some Lipan Apaches, and nobody ever worried about *them*. They weren't like other Apaches, like the Jicarillas or the Navahos. Lipans just didn't seem to want to fight.

So the Kiowa went on for eight sleeps, openly. They came to the place on Arrowhead River where the stones for chipping are, and some of the men wanted to gather a load then. But Bird-Tied-on-His-Head made them go on.

"We can pick up stones on the way home," he said. "They would just load us down and get in the way when we are fighting, if we take them now."

So the war party went on, and two days later, in the evening, the men saw the great mountains ahead of them against the sunset. Then they began to travel at night, by the one big fixed star that is the palm of Saynday's hand in the sky, with the stars that are his fingers revolving around it, slowly, all year, to watch over Saynday's world.

It was another four days before the Kiowas smelled smoke. There was a Ute village ahead of them, with the tipis just beginning to show in the dawn light. The Kiowas waited until just before the sun came over the rim of the world, and Bird-Tied-on-His-Head raised his hand and brought it down—*hard*—and the Kiowas swept forward in a charge.

The Utes were surprised, but they were good fighters, and not even the women were afraid. They stood behind the men and passed them arrows as they shot at the Kiowas.

The fight went back and forth, back and forth all morning. Then, when the sun stood right overhead, four Ute men had been killed, and the others turned and got on their horses, for the women had already broken camp, and gone away, slipping into the shadows under the great pines.

Buffalo Roars lay on the ground. He was not dead, but an arrow had gone right through him, below the chest, and another one had pierced clear through his leg. The Buffalo Doctor had the men kill a horse and skin it, so he made a splint out of the fresh rawhide for the leg. All he could do about the other wound was sing his power songs and pray.

The boys brought up the two gentlest horses the war party had. They made a sling out of the rest of the horsehide, and laid Buffalo Roars on it. Then the Kiowas started home, but they had to go slowly because of Buffalo Roars. In spite of everything the Buffalo Doctor could do, he was getting worse and worse, and was burning hot. Sometimes he even went out of his head for a time.

By the morning of the third day, when they were coming to the edge of the Plains, the Buffalo Doctor shook his head.

"I have done all I can," said the Buffalo Doctor as he finished his four sunrise songs. "If he isn't better by this evening, we'll have to go on and leave him."

"Leave my own brother!" Bird-Tied-on-His-Head exclaimed. "You can't ask me to do that."

"It is his life or everyone's," answered the Buffalo Doctor. "The Utes will catch up with us anytime, because we are so slow."

They hadn't thought Buffalo Roars could hear or understand, but now he opened his eyes. "Go on and leave me, my brother," he said, "I'm going to die anyhow. Don't waste the other's lives."

But Bird-Tied-on-His-Head could not leave his own brother lying out in the open that way. He sent the boys out to find a cave, and they did find one, on the mountainside. Bird-Tied-on-His-Head and the Buffalo Doctor brought the horse litter as close to it as they could, and then between them they half-carried, half-dragged Buffalo Roars into the cave. The boys had spread out some buffalo robes to make a bed and they laid the sick man on it. Everybody stayed in the cave with him, and it was a good thing they did, because a big Ute war party went past it right below them, looking for Kiowa tracks. On the hard rocks there were none to find, so the Kiowas were safe.

There was a strange animal smell in the cave, and the Buffalo Doctor said, "I think this must have been a wolf cave one time. It smells like it." And then everybody agreed that it did smell something like a coyote den, but stronger.

When it was full dark, before the late moon rose, Bird-Tied-on-His-Head pressed his brother's hand for good-bye. The war party went on, leaving Buffalo Roars with a gourd of water and some dried meat and mesquite meal beside him.

Perhaps it was that night, perhaps it was a later one. Buffalo Roars never knew for sure. He wakened, clear-headed and cool, but very thirsty. He felt beside him for the gourd of water, and found it. The gourd was about half full, so Buffalo Roars must have been awake before, and drunk some of the water.

Buffalo Roars turned a little, and outside the cave, forming a ring around its opening, he could see pairs of green sparks. At first he thought that evil spirits—owls—had come for him. He lay still and did not move, and the green lights did not move. They reminded him of something, and he remembered what it was: Coyote eyes!

"Oh, my brothers," said Buffalo Roars, stretching out his hand, "Do not hurt me. I'm a poor man, and very badly hurt. Have pity on me, and let me stay in your cave a little longer.

There was no sound, but presently one pair of green eyes moved out of the group and came forward. A great, gray-black bitch wolf stood over Buffalo Roars, and sniffed him all over. Then she stretched out beside him, so he could reach her teats, and he nursed like a puppy.

When he fell back on his robes, the mother wolf raised her head and faced her people. They all came forward to Buffalo Roars. One wise old male—he seemed to be the leader—sniffed and sniffed at the horse-hide splint. Then he began to chew it off.

After that, he licked and licked the injured leg, and the other wolves took turns licking Buffalo Roars's chest wound. He went to sleep, and when he woke again it was morning, and he was alone in the cave except for the old mother wolf, who was stretched out beside him and pressed against him like a dog, to keep him warm.

After that, the wolves cared for Buffalo Roars for a long time, until he was strong and well again. Even after he could get around, he stayed with the wolves. His brother had left him his bow and arrows, so when he could walk and shoot he went hunting. He killed game for the wolves to show them how grateful he was to them for helping him.

Buffalo Roars stayed there in the cave on the mountainside until spring came. Then he could walk like a strong man, and he gave the cave back to the wolves and started home.

The Kiowas were camped at the head of Arrowhead River, and when they saw the man coming from the west, they did not know him. Some thought he was a Ute, others thought he was a Navaho, and then Bird-Tied-on-His-Head came out of his tipi and looked.

"It is my brother! My brother we left to die!" He has come home to us!" And he ran out to greet Buffalo Roars.

When Buffalo Roars told them what had happened to him, the Kiowas were amazed. "Nah-nah-nah!" said his wives. "This is a wonderful thing."

"A wonderful thing indeed," said the Buffalo Doctor.

"The wolves have healed him when I could not. From now on, let his name be Gray Wolf, and his power be that of the wolf, for it is as strong as wildcat power, and he will be a great doctor."

And so Gray Wolf was, from that time on. And from that time on the Kiowas have honored the timber wolves, and called them brother and sister.

"Kiowa George" Poolaw, Kiowa

The Shaman's Spider

KIOWA

"Shaman" is a Siberian word, though which of many tribes coined it we do not know. It has become accepted anthropological slang for a certain kind of magic which can cause or cure disease.

Shamanism must be as old as man in the New World, for it is practiced everywhere from the Arctic Circle to Tierra del Fuego. The practice of shamanism is technically defined as disease-object intrusion and extraction. Mechanically, most shamans use some sleight of hand, as do our own stage and parlor magicians. Great dexterity is required in extracting the disease-causing objects in these cases, so that it will actually appear to bystanders to have been taken from the patient's body. Dancing, singing, and the use of drums or rattles may also be employed to distract attention.

In other cases—regarded as more serious in their effects—a physical object is not used. The patient is "shot" with a ray of sunlight or a moonbeam, and only finding out the identity of the opposing shaman, and killing him, will produce any cure.

"Wars" between shamans are not common among the Plains Indians, but do take place, particularly among the tribes in the northwestern part of the area. Perhaps the word "duel" would be more accurate to use, since only single individuals are usually involved. Among the Kiowa, however, there were shamanistic societies resembling those of the Northwest Plateau area, and the members of these societies were

145

*greatly feared because of the accumulation of power among the mem-
bership. However, a shaman did not need to be a member of a special
society, if he received a power-quest vision that made him a healer.*

*If a shaman's power is used to do harm—to kill or injure, or to steal
a lover, then, as with the Kiowa—it will cost the user the life of a
member of his family. Ultimately, of course, misuse of his power will
cost the shaman his own life.*

*When the power is used the shaman must be paid. His power will
have told him in advance what the objects given for his services are to
be, and whether he may keep them or give them away.*

*Whether a person is killed or cured by a shaman depends on his own
power to believe, and that of his tribe. Those natural skeptics, the
Comanches, seem to have scorned some shamanism, while other Plains
tribes took it with deep seriousness and credulity.*

The events in this story probably happened about 1800.

When this took place, the Out-on-the-Prairie-Band of Kiowas was
camped at the "breaks" of Palo Duro Canyon, in what is now known
as the Texas Panhandle, on the eastern edge of the Staked Plains. It
was a dangerous place to camp for long, long ago, the Comanches had
stuck yucca stalks in the dry ground across that dead level stretch of
land, beside the water holes, and only by following their stakes could
one travel across the wasteland. Naturally, the Comanches claimed the
Staked Plains as their own, but they were friends of the Kiowas and
the Out-on-the-Prairie-Band felt safe.

There was an Out-on-the-Prairie-Band war party out. They had gone
north, into the high mountain, where the Utes live. The Utes and the
Kiowas were always fighting. When the men had finished with the
Utes, they thought they might go south and see what the Navahos were
doing, and then come back east, across the Staked Plains.

The men were gone a long time, and the women moved the camp to
four different places along the edge of the canyon before the first scout
rode in.

"I thought I'd never find you," he said. "One of the men is hurt,
and I'll have to go back and tell them where you are."

"Can't the Buffalo Doctor help him?" one of the women asked. Like
every war party in those days, a Buffalo Shield Society member had
gone along to heal the sick and wounded.

"He's tried," said the young man, "but we think the Navahos put poison on the arrow that hit him; he's so hot and sick."

Everybody hurried around, then, to get the camp clean and in order. The caller went through from tipi to tipi, shouting that a healing doctor was needed. At nightfall, one man stood up and said,

"I will take out that poison."

Everybody felt better. He was a young man, and had only used his power a few times, but he might have the right kind, and succeed where the Buffalo Doctor had failed.

Just after dark, when the camp was settling down for the night, an owl flew over the camp, hooting.

"Oh," said one of the women, "that's bad. Perhaps he's dead. An owl brings death."

"Where did the owl come from, out in the open here?" her sister wondered. "Owls live in trees and brush."

"That makes it worse," answered the first woman.

But their husband was an Owl Shield member, and he could prophesy from what he heard the owl say.

"He's very sick, but he's not dead," he reassured his wives. "They'll be here tomorrow. Go and tell that young man to have all his curing things ready at daybreak, because he'll need them."

The two women went together to the young man's tipi. He was asleep, but his wife was awake and came out to talk to them.

"Tell him to get everything ready," the first wife said. "My husband heard an owl tell him the war party will be in tomorrow."

"He'd better take a sweat bath, too, and not eat anything," her sister added. That was in the days when Kiowa men married more than one woman if they could afford to. Usually they chose sisters, because they got along together better than strangers would.

Early in he morning, when the Owl Doctor and his wives got up, they saw the young man's wife and his friends had built a sweat lodge to spiritually clean the ground, and already were rolling red hot stones into it. He was getting all his power ready.

Then the war party came in when the sun was about in mid-sky. The sick man was tied to a litter between two horses. He was out of his head, and raving, and when his wives saw him, they began to wring their hands and mourn as if he were already dead. One of them even took her knife from her belt and cut off the tip of her little finger, to show the sorrow she felt.

"Where shall we take him?" asked the leader of the war party.

"Over here," said the young doctor's wife. Her friends had helped her build a brush arbor on the east side of the tipi, where the sweat lodge had stood earlier. That made it clean ground.

The men began untying the litter from the horses. They must have been Navaho horses to begin with. They were poor and scrawny, and stood with their heads hanging. When one of the herd boys came to take them away to pasture, they just plodded along behind them, as if they didn't know and didn't care. They didn't go galloping to the nearest clumps of grass as Kiowa horses would.

When the man was unloaded, the others laid him on the ground, where he thrashed around and shouted so that they were about to tie him again when the young doctor came out of his tipi.

"Don't tie him up," he said, "I can work better if he is free. First, I have to get the bandage off that wound in his leg. While I do that, build a little fire, and bring my pipe." When he had been obeyed, the doctor filled his pipe and smoked to the four world corners, four times.

It took him a long time to untie the buckskin bandage, and free the leg from the wooden splints the Buffalo Doctor had put on. Buffalo Doctors were the best ones for broken bones, so they usually used splints for whatever was wrong. This man's leg was not broken, but it was red and swollen, and pus oozed out of a great gash in the calf.

The doctor took a black silk handkerchief he had gotten from the Mexican traders the year before, and laid it over the wound. He looked and looked, and finally he said,

"I can see it. That Navaho shot him with spider poison. I'll have to get that poison out."

Then he began to shake his rattle and sing his power song:

> You, gray spider,
> Who hides in the rocks.
> Who lives at the bottom
> Of the great red canyon,*
> Look out, gray spider,
> I am coming to get you.
> Soon you will be gone
> And this man will be well.

He sang that song four times, and as he sang the sick man got quieter and quieter, until he lay quite still. Then the doctor took four

* Canyon de Chelly, Arizona

eagle-tail feathers, and began to brush the patient with them. He brushed from the top of his head to the wound; he brushed from the fingertips to the wound; he brushed from the soles of the feet to the wound, gathering all the evil in one place. He did this four times.

All the people were very still, even the herd boys, watching. They were all putting out their good thoughts to help the sick man, and watching him closely. Then the doctor got up and began to dance. He danced four times around the patient, and then he went four times around the brush arbor. One of the herd boys, who was watching the doctor instead of the sick man, thought he saw the doctor put something in his mouth the fourth time he danced around the arbor. Nobody else was looking at all.

The doctor came back, and stood over his patient on the east side.

"Now I can get it!" he shouted. He bent over the wound and began to suck. He sucked four times, and the last time he stood up and held out his hand, and spat a little gray rock spider into his hand. He threw it into the fire, and it shriveled up and was gone. Whatever the herd boy thought to himself, the sick man got better from that moment on.

George Hunt, Kiowa

PART 4

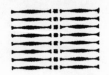 Freedom's Ending

A Bed for God

ARAPAHO

Missionaries to the Plains Indian tribes in the early 1900s were made of sturdy stuff. They had to be. If they had been in any way weak, if they had been willing to give up easily, they would have been betraying their God and themselves.

It was a hard struggle, uphill all the way, but not without victories in varying degrees. They gave enough encouragement to keep the missionaries going, as this story will show. The events in the story are true but the story itself has changed over the years from retelling. It is, however, a favorite mission folktale of many Indians in Oklahoma.

The small white-painted mission was set on a barren hill just west of Clinton, Oklahoma. There was the church, of course. There was a two-room frame house for the missionaries—husband and wife—to live in. And there was a one-room building that served for a school, which some of the Indian children attended more or less irregularly. Sometimes, in moments of exuberance, the missionaries talked of some day, maybe, just possibly, of adding two rooms, one for the boys and one for the girls, so the children could stay at the school without having to rely on their parents to bring them and take them home. It was a misty dream, however, for the local tribal leaders were opposed to schools in general and mission schools in particular.

153

So it was with some apprehension that the missionaries saw the local tribal leader come into the church one autumn Sunday. His name has been forgotten over the course of the years and now he is simply called Chief Big Shield.

He seated himself in the back and was very quiet, listening to hymns and prayers and sermon. After the service he approached the husband. They shook hands and exchanged a formal greeting.

"You do things nice in this church," Chief Big Shield observed. "You even have books to sing and pray out of, so people who know how to read won't get lost."

"Yes, we are very fortunate. The Mission Board in Washington was able to supply us with those books."

"Your church has an office in Washington?" Chief Big Shield asked thoughtfully.

"Yes," the husband replied. "There is a big stone church there and many people attend it. Some of those people are rich and they have been told about the Indians. They want to help the Indians. They thought perhaps if the Indians learned the white man's religion maybe the Indians would have a better life."

"Maybe so. I do not think that the Indians' religion is bad. But maybe so," Chief Big Shield pondered. "Maybe those rich people in Washington are right. Maybe if I learned your religion I would understand your ways better and I would be able to help my people more and keep my family from being hungry and cold. Maybe! Would you teach me your religion? After I have learned all about it, I will make up my mind which religion I like."

"Gladly," said the missionary. "My wife and I will both teach you and then you can tell your people the way we believe."

"No, you teach me alone. In the Indian way, a man teaches a boy and a woman teaches a girl. We do it in the Indian way."

"All right. We'll do it in the Indian way. When do you want to start?"

"I'll come to your house tomorrow morning. We start then."

"All right. You plan to stay all morning and my wife will cook dinner for us."

The following morning Chief Big Shield arrived at eight o'clock. The two men went into the little office that the missionary used as a study. And so it was for many mornings. Each day the wife would fix a noon dinner for them and then Chief Big Shield would leave for home.

It was a long, slow tedious job, with tales of the All Power matched to those of Father, Son, and Holy Ghost, but each man listened attentively to the other.

They came to the Christmas story. Chief Big Shield listened when the missionary told how Joseph had gone to the inn for a room and was told the inn was full but that he and Mary could use the stable. Chief Big Shield stopped the missionary at this point.

"You mean all the space they had for that poor woman to have her baby was in a livery stable like where we keep horses in town?"

"No, it was not like that. It was a barn with cows and chickens in it."

"That woman she had to give birth to that little baby lying on the floor?" Chief Big Shield wondered. "It was cold!"

"No. They made a bed for her of straw. It was warm in there, like a tipi. The animals helped make it warm. When the little Jesus was born His mother wrapped Him up in a blanket and He was warm and safe."

"It makes no difference if he was warm or cold. He should not have been born in a place where all those animals were. The women should have fixed him a tipi, like we do."

"There are no tipis in that country. The barn was a very safe place. In those days you had to be a man of some importance to even be allowed to stay in the barn. Joseph was a skilled man. He was a carpenter."

"I don't care what. They should not have let that woman have her baby there. You mean they don't have tipis in that country?" The missionary shook his head. Then Chief Big Shield continued. "We Arapahos do better than that. We think a lot of our children."

"Everybody for almost two thousand years has loved that baby and respected Him. His mother did everything she knew how."

"You keep talking about His mother trying. What happened to His father after His mother went into the barn? You know, the man His mother married?"

"God was His real father."

"Then why didn't God do something about it?"

"He did. He sent that little helpless humble baby to teach that the highest things are the lowliest."

Chief Big Shield got up and wrapped his blanket about him. He stood staring out the window towards the northwest. At last he spoke. "Each night we talk it all over good. We think we know you a little

better. Maybe! Just maybe we know you a little better now. Your religion is different from the Arapaho. It has some good things that we
can understand. But to treat a woman who is having a baby that way
is terrible. And to let the baby stay in a barn. That's bad. I go tell my
people. You say He came in December? December night, cold. He
ought to have a warm place to live. You say He come again?"

"Every December. Every Christmas, if you open your heart to
Him."

"I will go now. I'll tell all the people about this Baby being born in
a barn. I think, maybe this year we fix Him up right. Fix Him up
Arapaho way."

That day Chief Big Shield did not stay for dinner. He hurried away
leaving the missionaries in a bewildered state of mind. They hoped
they had not failed. If only they had given Chief Big Shield a little of
the Christian spirit they would be happy for Christmas.

The missionaries became more confused as the days moved nearer to
Christmas and the news of Chief Big Shield and other Arapahos
reached them. The Arapahos had received the money for rental of
their lands for grazing cattle. Chief Big Shield had gone to the furni-
ture store in Clinton and bought a bed—a magnificent brass bed. Other
Arapahos had brought bedding, pillows, and the ultimate—a glo-
riously striped trade blanket for a bedspread. And someone, no one is
quite sure who, contributed a tipi. The day before Christmas many
Arapahos left town on a pilgrimage to the northwest about ten miles
from Clinton, where there are some high bluffs. On the way out of
town they stopped at the mission and invited the husband and wife to
go with them. The missionaries were so curious that they could not
refuse.

Chief Big Shield led the way to the highest hill he could find on the
plain. The men carried the things from the wagon to the top of the
hill. The women erected the tipi and the men set up the brass bed. The
bed was made and a fire lighted inside the tipi. They all stood around
and admired the beauty of their work.

Chief Big Shield turned to the missionaries, "Now I say a prayer
for this new home and when I'm finished you say one in your way."

"I'll be glad to," replied the missionary.

"Now we go," the Chief said after the prayers were finished. "This
here tipi and bed is for baby Jesus. It will stay here all the time and
when the baby Jesus returns He will have a home. This year He is
fixed up good in the Arapaho way."

The two missionaries looked at each other in amazement. They had a convert!

"You will be a Christian?" the missionary asked.

"No. I stay an Arapaho. I like it that way. I just wanted to be sure that baby Jesus is warm each Christmas and that His mother has a place to stay. We, Arapahos, we like little children. You say baby Jesus' father is God, the Creator." The missionary nodded agreement. "Well, we believe in the Creator, too. We call him Maheo. So your God and our God will be pleased to take care of this baby. Maybe He represents all babies everywhere. We will celebrate all children's birthdays at your Christmas time."

And so the missionaries returned home with a glow in their hearts for the Christmas spirit. There on the high bluff stood the proud tipi looking like a woman with the glow of the fire burning like a candle in the night to tell of the love in the people's hearts.

Told by Richard Pratt, Arapaho
A different version was written by Zoe Tilghman and appeared in Oklahoma Today. *Published by the State of Oklahoma, Spring 1965.*

To Catch a Song

PAWNEE

The Pawnees hold an annual spring ceremony to renew the spirit of life and to thank God for good crops to feed the tribe. At that time they hold a big feast and play the ancient "hand game," which is a version of "Button, Button, Who's Got the Button."

The hand game is played all over the Plains in one form or another. It is usually a gambling game and so it is to the Pawnees when it is played socially. But in the spring the game is played ceremonially.

There are two pairs of tubular bone beads. One bead in each pair has a beaded or painted band around it. Two teams are pitted against each other. A pair of beads is given to two members of one team while the opposite team tries to guess in which hand the players hold the marked beads. The guesser uses a stick with a feather attached to it by a string to point to the chosen hands. Score is kept by moving special sticks, called counting sticks, from side to side on a table. Each stick represents a point for a correct guess.

In the ceremonial hand game of the Pawnee a special hand game set is used. The maker of the set is usually instructed throuyh a dream vision to make the set.

Special songs are sung while the guessing goes on. These songs are sacred and many of them are very old. These songs, too, are sometimes "caught" in a vision.

The following story happened in the mid-1960s at Pawnee, Oklahoma, and shows how one old woman brought the past into the present.

158

The Pawnee felt that a portion of their spring ceremonial hand game had been lost. The older people knew that long ago the old woman keeper of one of their sacred bundles was supposed to make new counting sticks each year, but no new ones had been made for many years.

Young men returning from military service wanted to perform the ceremony in the old way. They turned to the drum keeper of the tribe for help. But the drum keeper had never heard all the old songs. He took the young men, and the men who would sing to accompany their dancing, to an old man who had heard the songs when he was very young. They sat together during winter nights trying to recall the songs.

One night, in the early spring, when the first thunders come, an old, old lady, who was born in Nebraska, where the Pawnees originally lived, had a dream. The dream told her she must make the new counting sticks for the spring renewal ceremony and hand game. The dream told her how to fast, how to make offerings of tobacco, how to take a sweat bath, and lastly how to make the sacred sticks and attach the feathers to the calling stick.

The old lady sent for the drum keeper, and told him about her dream. She asked that he play the old songs for her. Sadly, he told her of the futile efforts the men had made to catch the lost words and music. The old lady told the drum keeper that she would pray and make an offering, and perhaps the songs would return.

For four days the old lady fasted and prayed. She grew weaker and weaker, but she refused to eat anything before the time was up. Finally, the four days were over. She sat sipping some warm soup, to break her fast, when the drum keeper arrived.

"I've come to tell you," he said. "Your prayers have been answered. They had great power. Last night Simon Yellowtail, the boy who was hurt in Viet Nam, he had a dream. All those songs we were looking for, they came to him. He come to my house and he sung all them songs for us. We sat up all night learning them songs. We can sing them real good now."

And so it was that God gave the Pawnee new counting sticks and returned their sacred songs.

Blanche Matlock, Pawnee

Home Cooking

KIOWA

One often wonders about the borderline between superstition and fact. It is safe to say that one man's superstition may be the next man's religion, but where does either border on the observable? In the story that follows there is no attempt to draw the line. We will let that inci-dent speak for itself.

We have already mentioned the Kiowa fear of bears. No more fright-ening being existed. To look at a bear, to be downwind of one—even to say the word "bear"—was absolutely taboo. A bear must be avoided, not killed.

The Kiowas lived in an area where bears were few and far between. Whatever the obscure tribal origins had been, the Kiowas must once have occupied an area where bears were plentiful. As their story of the Half-Boys shows, the bear was the great tribal enemy of the Kiowas. One of their sacred, secret women's societies was known as the Bear Women. The creature was never a subject of joking: It was always regarded with respect and dread.

━━━━━━━━━━

Kate could never understand her stepmother. Her own mother had died when Kate was twelve, so she had a clear memory of her quiet-ness, of the sureness with which she moved, and the seriousness with which she regarded life.

Mother had been dead four years when Father married Anne. Anne was half-white, and in many ways she was just the opposite of mother: quick and darting in her movements; always chattering—sometimes mockingly—and with a total disregard for anything serious.

When Kate was twenty, she married. It was clear to everyone that she and Anne would never get along in the same house, and she let Father arrange her marriage to Reuben, going to Reuben's father to suggest it; bringing Reuben's parents both home to meet Kate, and providing for the exchange of bridal gifts. Four horses Reuben's family brought, and in return Father gave them piles of blankets and sheets, and even some of Anne's prized patchwork quilts.

Anne was outspoken in the matter. "What do you think?" she demanded. "Do you have to make her bed when she's married? Do you have to tuck her in at night? She's a grown woman and she's going to have a husband to do that for her. And with *my* quilts!"

"Hush," father replied, soothingly. "She's your daughter, too. When you married me, you took my children with me."

"I did not!" Anne protested. "I took you, not a mess of snippy teen-agers."

"Well, now she's grown up, the way you said," Father reminded her. "Do you grudge any woman decent things to start her marriage with? You didn't have much when we were married, remember."

"That's right!" Anne retorted, and they were off on another of the endless wrangles that spoiled Kate's days, if not their own. She was glad to be getting married—to be getting away. In her own house perhaps she could have peace and quiet again.

As things turned out, it was a good marriage in all matters but one. There were no children. Kate and Reuben were happy together; they made a good living from their stock and horses, and they were generally regarded as a progressive young couple. Neighbors liked them and depended on them; Government boarding-school friends came to visit; they were prosperous. But they were alone together.

Anne did not let Kate forget that fact. "You got no children! You're just like an old mare in a pasture, getting fatter all the time and nothing to show for it. I should think you'd be ashamed! Me, I've got two families! One by my first husband, and three by your father. What kind of woman are you?"

Kate, as was her habit, tried to turn the subject.

"You said you'd show me again how to make pie crust," she replied.

Anne was flattered. Cooking was her strong point, and she knew it. Kate was competent in the kitchen, but no shining light. Anne began her instructions. Kate followed directions step by step, but still the crust did not turn out as light and flaky as the ones Anne made.

"Well, keep at it," said Anne, gathering her quilt pieces together and preparing to depart. "You may learn to make a pie yet, even if you can't make children."

Kate spoke to Reuben about it that evening.

"She's just a troublemaker, that's all she is," he reassured her. "She's jealous of you, and wants to make you unhappy."

"Don't you want children?" Kate asked.

"Yes," said Reuben, but if we can't have any of our own, we can always find some to adopt."

Kate was not satisfied. Adopted children would not be the same as her own, she feared. The next time the Field Nurse came by, Kate asked her if anything could be done by white doctors. The Indian doctors had no cure for barrenness, she knew.

"Well, there is something, but it's an operation that will have to be done in the hospital. It isn't always successful, but sometimes it works all right. What's the matter? Has your wicked stepmother been after you?"

"She isn't wicked. She's just . . . just mean," Kate said, in loyalty to Father.

"I think she has a wicked tongue," the nurse declared. "You think it over. Talk to your husband. If you want to, talk to your father. But if you can talk to him when Anne isn't around, that would be better."

"I'll see," Kate replied, deliberating.

"She did speak to Reuben that night, with the result that the next day he went to speak to Father, and on to the Agency to consult the Government doctor. When he returned that night, he told Kate, "They can do it, if you want to go through with it. And he says it may not work. You have to stay in the hospital a while, too."

Anne, when she heard what was being considered, was outraged. "First she didn't have any children because she wouldn't, and now she wants an operation so she can! Operations don't help! And just when I wanted to go to the North Country and you'd promised to take me, too!"

"We'll go," said Father reassuringly.

"Everybody knows that all you have to do to get children is want them! Some women even get children when they don't want them! She's just doing this to spite me!" Anne raged.

"We'll go," Father repeated.

So they went to the Black Hills, where some of the old, old people said the Kiowas had lived long ago, and as soon as they were on their way, Kate went to the hospital. Reuben took her and her suitcase in the car, and when he left her in the Agency town, to go back and see to the stock, he said, "It'll be all right. You'll see."

Probably it was, but it was all a blur to Kate. People talked to her, and put thermometers in her mouth, and bound a cloth tube tightly around her arm to take her blood pressure, they said, and stuck needles into her. The Field Nurse, whom she knew well, came in once or twice to see her, but most of the time she was besieged by strange women who just did things, without explaining, and by doctors who shook their heads or nodded them, and looked wise, but said very little.

Then one morning she woke up hungry. She hadn't been hungry for a long time, she felt. When the Nurse Aide came in with her tray, she sat up without help, and began to eat without encouragement.

But the hospital food was lifeless and dull, all pale gray or pale brown in color, without anything to make it appetizing. She did the best she could, but her taste for food was gone again. She thought of Anne's cooking, and of good meat, and gave up.

"You didn't drink your milk," the Nurse Aide stated when she came to take the tray.

"Milk's for babies," Kate replied.

"That's what you're here for, isn't it? Here, drink it."

Kate choked the colorless, lifeless fluid down somehow. She yearned for a good cup of coffee. When lunch came, there was fish on the tray.

"Don't you have any meat?" Kate asked longingly.

"It's Friday," said the Nurse Aide as if that answered everything, and left Kate to contemplate the unappetizing slab of halibut. Kate had eaten fish before, but not fish like this. Fried fish, crispy brown and hot from the skillet, not this whitish grayish blob.

For supper there was cream of tomato soup and crackers, with cottage cheese. The pale pink of the soup was encouraging, but it had no taste. Kate ate the crackers, and was ready to go home. She said so to Reuben when he came in the next day.

"I just lie here and think about how good a steak is when Anne fries it," she told him. "I wish she was back. I'd do about anything to get a good piece of meat—even dried meat."

"She'll be back Monday," Reuben answered. "I'll tell her what you said. And the doctor says you can go home pretty soon anyway, so you can fry a steak for both of us."

Tuesday afternoon Anne came in. "I heard you was asking for me," she began. "How do you feel?"

"All right now," Kate answered. "They let me walk up and down the hall, and sit in the chair, and they say I can go home next week."

"Reuben told your father you wanted same dried meat," Anne continued.

"Oh, I do! I think one reason I'm kind of weak and slow is that I'm hungry all the time."

"Well, I brought you some."

Anne reached for her bag, on the floor beside her.

"I brought it from the North Country," she said. "Some Crows gave it to us." She brought out a small paper-wrapped package, and extended it. Kate opened the package. The meat was darker in color than any dried meat she remembered having seen, and it smelled stronger.

"Those Crows must dry meat different from us," Kate said dubiously.

"It's all right," Anne reassured her. "They do most things different from tribes around here."

Kate bit into the meat; the taste, too, was stronger than dried beef, but she ate it all. "It tastes wild," she said when she finished.

Anne sat back in the chair and looked at Kate. "You got it all down," she observed. "It was wild. You know what you were eating? Bear meat!"

Kate sprang out of bed and gazed at her stepmother with horror. "You brought me bear meat!" she gasped. "You witched me! Oh, you are cruel! Now I'll never have any children—not ever!"

Anne's lips curled in a malicious smile. "That's what I meant to happen," she drove her point home. "You tried to keep me from going to the North Country. I got even." And she took her bag and departed.

Kate, weak, shaky, and prone to outbursts of tears, went home with Reuben the next Saturday. She told him what had happened.

"That's all right," he reassured her. "We'll adopt some children; lots need better homes than they got."

"They'll never be the same as our own," Kate sighed.

And although she accepted, cared for, taught, and educated ten, she never managed to think of them as hers.

Berdina Kodaseet, Kiowa

The Candy Man

KIOWA

The Kiowa, like all Plains Indians, have certain well-established customs that have their beginnings in the far past, perhaps even before the development of the classic Plains culture.

The custom of having a spokesman is one such survival. A man or a woman never speaks for himself or herself; instead, another person speaks for them. This custom was followed very closely when dealing with white people, and often gave the men from Washington the idea that a speaking chief had complete control over his people and made all the decisions. This was not the case, however. A decision, in theory anyway, had to be approved by all the people or there was no decision. That such unanimous agreement could be reached was an ideal rather than a fact; oftentimes decisions could never be reached.

The spokesman is still present today, not only when people deal with the government but in their social life. At any modern Indian gathering the spokesman may be seen and heard. He may be the announcer for the entire event or he may be a friend of the person who wishes to be heard.

The spokesman is very important in the long-established giveaway. A giveaway is a sort of social security. An older person and his family can give away goods in honor of a younger person. A family may choose to honor a young man who has just graduated from high school or college. They will call in all their relatives, who will contribute money and gifts.

The family will give to the old and the poor people in the tribe, and to visitors from other tribes. The reasons for holding a giveaway are endless, as are the gifts given. There are always dress lengths of fabric for the women, blankets, shawls, money, and even today, sometimes a horse. At one Indian gathering a man who lived in the city received a horse and had a very hard time finding a home for it.

The family and their spokesman gather in front of the speakers' stand. The drummers play the family song, and all people wishing to honor the family move with them around the dance circle. Then the spokesman will speak, telling all the people the reason the family is having a giveaway. The head of the family, either man or woman, tells the spokesman whom to call to receive presents. The spokesman can either call the person himself, or he can request that the Master of Ceremonies do it. The Master of Ceremonies of today, with his loudspeaker and microphone, replaces the camp crier of the past.

The story that follows has much of the past mixed with the present. It is a true story, but because of the love of the Kiowa for the Candy Man it is now part of their modern folklore. The Candy Man has died since this incident took place in the late 1950s, but his memory will always live with the Kiowa.

The Gourd Dance Society had been long forgotten after the Kiowas took the white man's road. But the young servicemen returning from World War II and Korea kept asking the older people to remember the past; to bring all the good things from it back to the Kiowas, to restore their heritage and to make them feel like Kiowas in their turn.

At last everything that could be remembered had been retold, and the pieces were coming together. The young men asked their elders to hold a Gourd Dance. Through a whole winter the old men planned and they all rehearsed, until the younger men knew exactly what they should do.

A place to hold the dance had to be selected, and the town of Carnegie, Oklahoma, was the unanimous choice. It was in the center of the Kiowa lands, and it was known as an Indian town, as opposed to the Agency town, a few miles east. There was a public park at Carnegie, and the city fathers were willing to allow the Kiowas to use it for an entire weekend. The time was to be the Fourth of July, and, although no one mentioned it, that was about the time when the Kiowas used to hold their Sun Dance.

A delegation visited the commanding officer at Fort Sill, and requested permission from him and the director of the Post Museum to borrow back the sacred shield, the staking spear, and the war bonnet of one of the ancestral members of the society, which had been placed in the museum for safekeeping. In addition, they requested the bugle that White Bear had captured from the army in the 1870s. They also wanted a bugler, wearing a uniform of the period, to play the instrument. All their requests were granted.

Carnegie City Park, beside the sluggishly flowing Washita River, was an oasis. It was shadowed by high old trees, live oak, elm, cottonwood, and "the biggest chinaberry tree in the world," to quote the Chamber of Commerce. The earth was bare but hardpacked, and it was sprinkled with water from time to time, so there was little dust. The sun-dappled dance ring, surrounded by tents and campers, all facing inward, as in the Sun Dance circle, was large enough to hold a crowd, even in the heat, without making anyone feel uncomfortable.

Little girls in their best dresses darted back and forth like swallows, while their older sisters, helmeted with hair curlers, sat solemnly on the benches, chewing their gum and watching. The Gourd Dancers formed a mass of color at the west side of the ring representing their place in the tipi—the place of honor and guardianship. With them sat the society's sister, serene and regally beautiful in white buckskin. Only members of the society would dance during the afternoons, and only selected drummers might sing. The evening dancing would be "open"—all might take part.

Sunday afternoon was the climax of the ceremony. Indian people had come from all over the state, many of them friends or relatives of the Gourd Dancers. Others were sightseers, who had heard that the Kiowas were reviving an old and honored society, and had come to watch the great event.

At intervals in the afternoon there were many giveaways to honor young men who had served in the army, navy, or air force. Gifts were given to the visitors, to the aged, and to the poor. The announcer, through a microphone, called the people, one at a time, to come and receive their gifts, and one at a time they came forward, ceremoniously shook hands with the young man being honored and with his family, and returned, laden, to their seats.

All afternoon the bugler, a black man selected in honor of the Buffalo Soldiers, played every cavalry call in existence, from reveille to taps. Firecrackers being set off in the adjoining amusement park blended with the tooting whistle of a miniature train on which the children rode with shrieks of laughter and with the bugle calls and the drumming and singing that accompanied the dancing.

Late in the afternoon a special giveaway was announced. Everyone watched as one of the oldest and most dignified chiefs made his way to the microphone. Surely he would not speak for himself! Surely he would let the announcer be his spokesman! But the old man took the microphone and waved the announcer aside. He began to speak in Kiowa, and when he had finished the announcer translated his words.

"I'm here to be the spokesman for my friend, the Candy Man. I don't know if any of you young people know about the Candy Man. Him and me, we growed up together, and when he married, he brought his wife here and they opened a candy store. My! It was a good store. Every time one of us Kiowas come in there, he gave us some candy. Free. He listened to our troubles and he helped us. I wrote to him where he lives now, in Texas, and told him what us Kiowas are going to do today, so he came. He wants to talk to you."

The old chief gave the microphone to a short, elderly white man. He was dressed in a black suit and tie, and a stiffly starched white shirt. He spoke slowly, as if the words had to be pulled out of his throat.

"I come here today to see my good friends. Most of you I haven't seen for a long time. It is good to be home in Oklahoma; in the Kiowa country. I haven't been back since my wife died. I came today because I wanted to thank all the Kiowa people for what they have done for me.

"Back a few years, my candy store burned to the ground. My wife and I lived behind the store, and all our own things were lost. We'd never been able to save much, and now we had just nothing. Our children were all grown up and had gone away.

"But the Kiowas came, young ones and old ones. They brought us food, clothing—all the things we needed to start our home again. My friend here, the chief, he took us into his home and his wife nursed my wife when she was sick.

"After my wife died, I went to live with my son, in Texas, but I've never forgotten how good the Kiowas were to me.

"I can't give away any fancy presents. I'm not a rich man, but my wife and I always wanted to have enough candy on hand so we could give each Kiowa child a sackful. Here in these boxes are sacks full of candy for all the children who are here today. May God bless all of them and all of you.''

The Candy Man shook hands with his old friend, and the two embraced. The singers began a special song to honor their friend, the Candy Man. Indians and non-Indians together remembered the good things from the past and watched the children enjoy their gift.

Carol K. Rachlin, personal observation

The Forty-nine Songs

INTERTRIBAL

No book of this kind would be complete without reference to, and inclusion of, some of the Forty-nine songs, which are modern Indian folksongs. These are sung all over the Plains and at many Indian gatherings throughout the United States.

The connotations of Forty-nine dancing and singing are those of a courting dance, although it is a social dance in which all ages participate. After the formal dancing for an evening is finished, young people, and some older ones, return to their tents, change their dance costumes for blue jeans or house dresses, and return to the dance ring.

Here the dancers form a line, men and women alternating, around a group of drummers. The musicians are equipped with a hand drum, on which four or five men beat with short drumsticks, and to which they and the dancers sing. The dancers' hands, linked with each other, circle the drummers in an ever-tightening ring, until the dance becomes a circle packed as close to the drummers and the dancers as possible.

Origins of the Forty-nine dances and songs are obscure. We have been told by very old people that it started in the year of the California gold rush, 1849, from which it derives its name. White people were crossing the northern Plains from east to west, and, inevitably, crossing Indian lands and killing Indians and buffalo alike.

The Plains Indians had felt insecure for some years previously, and they did what they usually do when they are worried: They danced.

And because they did not want to be disturbed, they danced at night, with as little noise and light as possible. In fact, at first, it was most probably a protest dance rather than the courting dance of today.

The songs are informally made up by the participants. A new song will be picked up quickly and passed orally from tribe to tribe. The popular songs continue to be sung for years. Each song is sung four times, which is the sacred number of the Indians.

Here are some of the songs that are most frequently sung in English interspersed with nonsense syllables, in the night dance.

You know that I love you, Sweetheart,
But every time I turn around
You always say you got another one.
You know God-damn good and well
That I love you.
* * *
When the dance is over, Sweetheart,
I will take you home
In my one-eyed Ford
* * *
She got mad at me,
'Cause I said hello
To my old-timer,
But that's just okay with me.
She don't like me
'Cause I drink whiskey.
But that's okay with me,
I got 'nother one.
* * *
Although you're living with another,
It's only you and no one else
I'm thinking of.
Someday our dreams will all come true,
And then you'll be mine,
Be mine from now until eternity.
* * *
I'm from Oklahoma,
Got no one for my own,
So I come here looking for you.
If you'll be my honey
I'll be your sugar pie.
I'm from Oklahoma,

Got no one for my own,
So I come here looking for you.
If you'll be my snag,
I will be your snaggaroo.
* * *
See you next summertime,
Crow Rodeo and Indian Fair.
We'll dance the Forty-nine
All night long.
See you next summertime,
Lake View Pow-Wow Amusement Park.
We'll ride the Tilt-a-Whirl
All night long.
See you next summertime,
American Indian Exposition.
We'll dance and sing the Forty-nine,
All night long.
Hope you don't catch the diarrhea,
All night long,
All night long.
* * *
I don't care if you've been married fifty times,
I love you, darling.
I don't care if you've got fifteen children,
I'll get you yet.

And finally, a short song of the militant American Indian movement, started in the 1960s, referring to the B.I.A., or Bureau of Indian Affairs of the United States Department of the Interior:

B.I.A., I'm not your Indian any more.
You belong to white man now,
So farewell, good-bye to you, honky.

Louellen Brown, Oto, age seventeen

How Much Can Be Lost?

CHEYENNE

In 1951 the question was raised at a museum meeting: How can one distinguish between northern and southern Cheyenne arts and crafts? Everyone present was familiar with the exquisite work in quill and beads done by southern Cheyenne women; many of us had seen specimens recovered from the northern Cheyenne battlefields such as Sand Creek and Beecher's Island, but once the problem was posed no one present could recall seeing any northern Cheyenne work of recent vintage.

One of us took the question home from the meeting, which was held in Denver, and consulted a famous beadworker, Mary Inkanish, one of the southern Cheyenne. What was northern Cheyenne beadwork like?

"Nah," said Mama Inkanish. "You forget something you got to remember. All you arts and crafts people do. Northern Cheyennes, they got no crafts."

"No crafts! When the French explorers came into the Lakes country in 1540, or thereabouts, one of their duties was to send specimens of Indian work back to France so the princes would know what kind of people lived overseas. They were sealed in lead boxes and stored away until somebody cleaned out the palace attics after World War II, and they're still there, in Paris, in a special museum. And the greatest of them are Cheyenne. That was before the tribe divided. The northern Cheyenne had to have arts and crafts."

"You forget," said Mama gently. "All you museum peoples forget. Crafts is made by living peoples. Crafts is alive. I know. For a long time them northern Cheyennes, they don't have nothing to live for. My mother told me. She was there, some of the time. I still got relatives living up there."

"You have? Would you like to visit them?"

"I guess," Mama considered. "I never did see none of them myself; I never did see that North Country they say is so beautiful."

"If I can get the money for the trip, will you come with me?"

"Sure I come. Be ni-i-i-i-ce, seeing that North Country."

One of the ironies of field anthropology is that while it is not difficult to get funds for large study projects, extending over months and years and thousands of miles, which often are never fully written up, it is hard to raise money for such a simple thing as going from Oklahoma to Montana to compare northern and southern Cheyenne arts and crafts.

The first step was a letter to the late, great Frederic H. Douglas, head of the Department of Native Arts at the Denver Art Museum. He knew Mama, and loved and respected her as did most of her "museum peoples" friends.

"I have a small trust fund set up in memory of my parents for just this kind of thing," Dr. Douglas wrote in reply. "If you can use a thousand dollars this summer, you're welcome to it. Better stop here on your way north, so you and Mama can check over the collection and pick out what you want to take to Lame Deer to show the people.

So we were really going to Lame Deer, Montana. A landscape painter friend, Martha, accompanied us, and we set out to learn about northern Cheyenne arts and crafts and, incidentally, about the how and why of the making of legends from static history.

I have written this highly personal account to answer the questions of those who want to know how it is done; how such information is collected, and how can you trust people to tell the truth. Simply because, over a period of years, you have to know and trust and love each other.

◆━━━◆◆━━━◆

Mama lived in Anadarko. We picked her up, with numerous small suitcases, bags of presents for the northern relatives, a pair of moccasins she had made for Dr. Douglas—fortunately, as it turned out, they fit him, for that towering man had surprisingly small hands and feet.

"I like go by way of Colony," Mama suggested when we were under way.

Well, Colony was only a little way off the main route, and it is a pretty place, so we turned off there.

"That where I go to school," Mama said, indicating a gaunt and gutted brick building. "I run away from home to go to school. You want to see where I run away from, at Darlington Agency?"

Again a change of route was indicated, but the few miles of red dust between Colony and Darlington would bring us back close to the main highway. The Agency there was gone, and of the original buildings only the "Employees' Club" was standing. The state had taken over the place as a game farm, and we were confronted by signs that read, "This is nesting season. Please do not disturb the pheasants."

"All Cheyennes run away from here sometimes," Mama stated matter-of-factly.

We had read of the northward trek of half the tribe, in 1878–79, but this seemed to bring it closer to home than any printed page could.

"Were any of your family on that trip, Mama?" Martha asked.

"Some. Three of my mother's sisters. Two died on the way. My mother wasn't born then, but my grandma, she tell me about it."

"Did your grandmother go?"

"No. She expectin' my mother, so she don't go."

Always, when Mama talked of old days and old ways, her careful government school English slurred into trading post speech.

"Can you tell us about it?" I asked.

"I tell you what I hear my grandma tell. You know they bring the Cheyennes down here after that Custer kill? The Crows was the ones gave the Cheyennes away.

"Well, it was in the fall. Pretty cool nights, but warm days. And they put them here at Darlington, and say, 'This where you stay. You get rations here. Go to work. No more buffalo hunting, no more fighting.' "

I started the car and headed back for the highway.

"Was all open country then. The Cheyennes could look around every way. No mountains. No rivers. Just that ole muddy red Canadian river. They make camp in the bend, right here."

We stared at the spot, indistinguishable to our eyes from the surrounding miles of grassland.

"Winter come. Was co-o-o-o-o-ld. Nothing to break the wind and it blow, it blow all time. So they say to each other, 'Is better off at home, where there're mountains to break the wind.'

"But still they stay because the government told them to. Rations was short. What was given to the southern Cheyennes before, now everybody has to share. So nobody has enough, and the children gets skinny, and their little bellies puff out, they so hungry. And then people start to get sick. That coughing sickness—newmornia, you call it?

"So some of the men went to the Agent. He was a Quaker, John Miles. Good man, but he make everybody mind him. But this time he scared of them Cheyennes, they so mad. And they say, 'You let us go on buffalo hunt.' And Miles say, 'In spring, when country open up.' And Dull Knife, he just laugh and say, 'In spring we all be dead.' But they went back to the camp and tell the women Agent say in spring they can hunt.

"Little Wolf, he was the one. Little Wolf and Dull Knife, they the chiefs. And they go away somewhere, and Little Wolf say, 'My friend, in the spring, when we go hunting. we run away.'

"And Dull Knife say, 'All right.' But when spring come and they go out on those Comanche Staked Plains west of here, the soldiers go with them, so they don't get a chance to run away.

"After they get back, it rain, and the river overflow and make little sloughs, and the sloughs fill up with mosquitoes, so everybody have shakes and fever. They only got a few buffalo, and they eat them right up, so pretty soon everybody hungry again. And Dull Knife say to Little Wolf, 'My friend, if we don't go home, pretty soon no Cheyennes left.' So they start to make their plan to go back north."

Mama's head was nodding, and her eyes closed, as we continued into the dusk. Then she woke, refreshed, and when we pulled into a motel for the night, she ate a hamburger with relish and slept the night through like a baby. In the morning we went on, across the Staked Plains and northward.

The three days we spent in Denver were busy. The entire Cheyenne collection had to be picked over and sorted, and a selection of the best specimens made. We finally decided on a man's costume with bands of soft yellow quillwork on it; a woman's dress of white buckskin with transverse bands of blue and white beadwork across the shoulders, and a set of horse trappings. Lack of space forbade our taking the saddle, but we took a beaded saddle blanket and bags, a German silver bridle, braided reins, and a short, braided curt, or short whip, with a beaded handle.

As time went on, it began to look as if we had acquired a Cheyenne department store, for Dr. Douglas kept adding to the assortment: Belts with German silver conchas, knives in beaded cases, feather fans with beaded or quilled handles, rattles to match—on and on the inventory grew, until I was dizzy with the effort of listing, and Mama and Martha ready to drop from packing and sorting. It had to go with us, for where we were going there were no railroads, no buses, no public transportation of any sort.

"Stop!" I exclaimed finally. "We haven't room for another thing, not even a scalp."

"Don't you want a scalp?" inquired Dr. Douglas wistfully. "I have some beauties here, and some of them have never been identified." He took a box down from a high shelf, and set it on the table. The lid, when lifted, revealed a generous assortment of scalps. Mama reached over and picked up the top one. She examined it thoroughly and then dropped it in disgust.

"Nits!" she announced. "Must be Crow."

"Well, that's one identified anyhow," said Martha.

And I added, "No, thank you. No scalps."

From Denver the road shoots almost straight northward to Sheridan, Wyoming. In the cool of the morning we set out, and Mama gazed about her happily. "Mountains," she said. "Do we go by Fort Robinson?" Again it was a little off the beaten path, but we detoured.

"This where they come to," she informed us. "All across Kansas, Nebraska, they walk, walk till they get here."

Fort Robinson was being restored, and it is now a job of restoration any historical society could be proud of. Mama looked at the stone walls of the guardhouse. Her chin quivered, and tears ran down her cheeks. "Oh, my poor people," she wept. "So cold, so hungry, so tired, and they shut them in there and when they tried to break out those old soldiers killed them. They got away, though," she added proudly. "Some of them got clear away and got home." And she wept.

Speechlessly, we reentered the car and resumed our way. History—living spoken history—was very close around us.

In Sheridan, that night Mama asked, "Which way we go now?"

"Straight north and then east," I answered, studying the road map.

"We go near the place that Custer got killed?"

"Yes, right by it."

"We stop?"

"If you want to."

The Custer battlefield is a national monument and beset with tourists. Mama paid no attention to them as Martha stopped the car on the crest of the rise. She scrambled out and stood looking around her. "I show you something," she informed us. "Then I tell you something. If I'm right about one, I be about the other, ain't it?"

"Surely," I said, following her over the eastern slope. Martha already had sketch pad and colored pencils out, and was making notes of the landscape for a later painting.

"Now," said Mama, "they say was one soldier ran away from the fight, but the Cheyennes saw him and killed him off by himself. Somebody tole me they put a marker on that place."

And sure enough, a quarter of the way down the slope, in a little ravine where a man might hope to hide and be safe, was a grave marker: "Private, Unknown. Killed in the Battle of the Little Big Horn, June 25th, 1876."

"There, you see," Mama insisted, "I tell you the truth."

We turned and trudged back up the slope. The summer sun was hot. As we reached the crest, Mama turned to me. "You got knife? Mine's in the car."

"Yes," I replied, slightly bewildered. I took a two-inch penknife out of my purse and handed it to her. She felt the blade gingerly. "Pretty dull," she said, but she kept it.

Then, with a blood-curdling scream, she leapt on unsuspecting Martha who had her back turned to us. "I get you, you old Custer you! You Yellow Hair who rob the Cheyennes!"

Martha's hair was gray, and anyone who looked less like Custer in his heyday would be hard to imagine. She was utterly bemused. Mama cut off a small lock of her hair and put in in her handbag.

"Now, you see, I was right about that other, and I'm right about this," she triumphed. "Was a woman killed Custer, one of the sisters of his Cheyenne wife. She kill that Yellow Hair because he disgrace all the Cheyenne women. Maybe next I get a Crow." She looked at my red hair teasingly.

Suddenly, we all realized that we were a source of innocent merriment to an ever-increasing crowd of tourists, and fled to the car.

"We go to Crow Agency. Is on the way," Mama decided as we left the monument. "I got a cousin lives there."

"Who is that?" I inquired.

"She the granddaughter of my grandmother's sister. The one that live through that trip from Darlington. She never go back."

"What's she doing at Crow Agency?" Martha demanded. "I thought the Cheyennes didn't think much of the Crows." That scalp was still lurking in the back of her mind, I knew.

"We don't," Mama answered briefly, "but that's where her husband lives."

"Is he a Crow?"

"No. He's a white man. She wouldn't marry a Crow. He have a trading post there."

So we descended on Crow Agency, and the cousin, who took us in and fed us canned chicken and hot buttered toast and a pot of tea, together with fried bread and wild plum jam and pounded dried meat —all served on Spode dinnerware. Martha and I exclaimed over the dishes, and the cousin opened cupboard after cupboard of the finest English wares and displayed them.

"We're just a hundred miles from the Canadian border," she explained, "so when my husband goes up to buy things for the post, or to see his relatives, I can go shopping for dishes and get just enough at a time to bring them in duty-free."

Afterward we sat outdoors and watched the sunset from the garden, and never in my life, not even in southern Oregon, have I seen such a garden. Delphiniums stood six feet tall. Gladiolas were as high. Roses, plate-sized petunias, and huge nicotiniana bushes made a potpourri of fragrance all about us. And at the far end, beyond the rose hedge, were the kitchen garden and the herb garden, with the sweetness of rosemary and thyme and mint.

When we left for Lame Deer the next morning we managed to squeeze a bushel of fresh vegetables and a box of heavy-sweet herbs into the car, though I have never been quite sure how we did it.

The multicolored hills rolled past us, and in midmorning we looked out from the top of one and saw Lame Deer in the valley below us. I have seen many agency towns, but Lame Deer was one unto itself. At the north end of the valley was the usual cluster of white-painted cigar boxes that denote Agency buildings and employees' residences. A straggle of log cabins—government built—spread along the valley from the Agency to a knot of wooden shacks, one with a sign proclaiming it to be a trading post, the other proudly announcing itself as the Lame Deer Hotel. On the opposite side, facing us, was an enormous red brick building, apparently abandoned, which could have been anything from a school to a warehouse.

"Well," I said as we began the descent, "we'd better check at the Agency."

Unlike many of his peers, the Agent was charming and cooperative. He had been alerted to our coming by a call from the Bureau of Indian Affairs Area Office in Denver. We were expected, and, as he frankly said, it was a pleasure to look at some new faces occasionally.

When the amenities had been disposed of, I inquired about the hotel. Could we get rooms there?

"I suppose you could," he said thoughtfully, "but I'm not sure you'd want to. My wife and I talked about that this morning. We think the best place for you to stay is the hospital. The generator's still working so you could have lights, and there's running water—not hot, but water—and inside plumbing. One of the refrigerators still connected, and we'll lend you a hot plate so you can cook. You'll get better food and be quieter that way. The Forestry Service crew's taken over the north end of the building, but you can have the south end and never see or hear them—unless you want to."

My adult working life had been spent in and out and roundabout Bureau of Indian Affairs agencies, but this was a new setup.

"Aren't there any patients in the hospital?" I asked.

"Not any more," said the Agent cheerfully. "We had to shut it down in 1944, when the furnace gave out and we couldn't get repair parts. I was in Europe then, in service, and the man who came out from Washington to take over temporarily just didn't seem to cope. He let pipes burst because he didn't know they had to be drained— things like that."

"But there's running water now . . ."

"Oh, yes, but you'll have to heat it yourselves. And there are beds. We had to burn the bedding, though, after the rats got in it, except for a few of the mattresses. But I think you can get whatever you need at the trading post, and my wife will help you out."

"Thank you," I said feebly, and we wandered out to the car and drove to the hospital.

The south end consisted of a twenty-bed ward and a laboratory with

a refrigerator, with a bathroom opening off it. Adjoining these were
the head nurse's quarters—a small, barren bedroom with its own bath.
Mama promptly claimed that space.

Martha and I were left with the twenty-bed ward. Each of us established herself in a corner; Martha with paints and brushes and folding
easel, and I with the inevitable typewriter and portable file. The center
space we determined to use as a living room.

We went to the trading post. Enamelware plates, cups, bowls, and
saucers. The cheapest possible tableware. A skillet and a cooking pot,
with spatula and spoon. And finally, almost as an afterthought, two
thin blankets apiece, six towels and face cloths, and some sheets that I
believe were made of plywood. I am still using them, twenty years
later. They are no softer.

On our return to the hospital, we found a huge, chunky young Cheyenne man waiting for us. On his shirt shone the brightest brass star I
have ever seen anywhere.

"I'm the policeman," he announced. "Mrs. Agent, she sent you
them things." He gestured toward a table loaded with a hot plate and
the minimum in cooking equipment to supplement what we had
bought.

Mama peered up at him. She was a tiny woman. "What's your
name?" she asked.

"Delbert American Horse," he informed her.

"You my cousin!" Mama cried delightedly, and embraced him.

"I unload the car," he said, disentangling himself, and did so.

Soon, it seemed, we had only begun the collecting of Mama's relatives. In two days, it appeared that she was related to every one in
Lame Deer and the environs. When Delbert observed that we had
neglected to buy food at the trading post, and our sole supply at the
moment consisted of not-quite-so-fresh vegetables from Crow Agency,
he sent his wife over with a pot of coffee and a slab of venison. That
night he went hunting and thoughtfully presented us with an entire
deer.

We observed the whole process of preparation the next morning,
when Mama skinned and butchered the deer and began peeling the
meat from the bones of the hind legs to dry in the sun. She sent me off
for cheesecloth and a clothesline from the trading post, and began
draping the venison over the line, then covering it with the cheesecloth

to dry. As soon as people saw what she was doing, other older women joined her and they all worked cheerfully together, chattering in Cheyenne like birds chirping at the sunrise. She prepared to scrape and dry the hide.

It was a magic summer. We went to the northern Cheyenne Sun Dance, the northern Arapaho Sun Dance, and to the Crow Sun Dance. At the latter, the Sun Dance priest set the end of his whistle against the center pole and a stream of water miraculously poured out to further tantalize the dancers.

Martha painted and painted—the tawny red hills, the towering buttes, the winding blue course of Tongue River—while Mama and I visited and were visited by an endless stream of relatives, all curious to see this guest from the south.

Always there were the stories of the flight north from Darlington; of the bitter cold, the endless flatness of the short-grass country, and of those who died on the way and were left behind in unmarked graves.

And nowhere, anywhere, in trading posts or homes, were there any arts and crafts. It was unbelievable! I had never known Indian homes without at least a feather fan on view. There were not even beads in the posts, and, while sinew was abundant, it was not used for bead-work or sewing moccasins, but was thrown away. Only Mama thriftily gathered up, dried, and preserved every slab of it she could. And she began to tan every hide she could get her hands on.

I took the matter of crafts up with the Agent. He knew why we had come, of course, and Lame Deer was not precisely a summer resort. But he could offer no suggestions at first. After much consideration he said, ''Suppose I give you a room at the Agency, and you put up a display of the things you brought from Denver? The people will enjoy seeing them, and it just may start some of the old ladies remembering.''

I leapt at the idea like a fish going after a fly. The next morning we went to work. The first thing to do was to make sure there was a lock on the door of the room we were going to use. The Agency itself was locked at night, but it was just as well to avoid taking unnecessary risks with someone else's beadwork. When we made sure the room could be secured, we started hanging things on walls and laying them on tables. And we discovered that Dr. Douglas had slipped one over on

us after all. At the bottom of the footlocker in which we had brought
the specimens was a magnificent eagle-feather war bonnet. Perched on
a hat rack, it was the finishing touch.

When we at last opened the door, late that afternoon, the people
began edging in. First the older women, for this was women's work
and they were Mama's contemporaries and relatives. Later came the
younger women and the men, and, finally, the school children.

At first they stood and looked, without speaking. Then, furtively,
some fingered a fringe. Someone else ran a finger over a strip of beadwork, marveling at the evenness of its flat rows of small matched
beads. And then the questions began.

"Who made these? Could Cheyennes ever have done such work?
How did we know Cheyennes made them? Could anyone do that kind
of work now?"

"I can," said Mama. She sent Martha back to the hospital for the
little tin skate box without which she never went anywhere, and from
it took out beads, sinew, a deer hide she had tanned while we were in
Lame Deer, and began a demonstration. The women crowded around
her, watching, wondering, as she slipped her awl beneath the outer
layer of hide, lifted, and inserted a sinew thread on which to string the
beads. Back and forth her steady hands went, never hurrying, always
moving, until she had a strip of beadwork about six inches long and
three rows of six beads each wide.

"You try," she said, handing the work and the tools to Delbert's
mother, and, fumblingly, the other woman tried to repeat her movements. I looked up, and saw the Agent in the doorway. His eyes, like
mine, were misted with tears. He jerked his head backwards and we
went outside.

"Do you know where we can get beads?" he asked. "We have the
hides and the sinew, if she shows the other women how to work them."

"I'll write to Denver . . ." I began, not knowing any nearer place
for supplies.

"Write, nothing!" said the Agent. "You've got another month to
go here, and she can teach them a lot in that time. You come on in my
office and phone."

The supplies arrived with the mail, three days later. That was the
day my letter would have gone out. Mama undertook the distribution
and the Agent's secretary and I the bookkeeping. We worked on the
principle of "Make two and keep one," and the articles returned were

the nucleus of an arts and crafts cooperative and a small sales counter in the Agency. I had never worked so hard at such a job when I was paid to do it.

And when we packed to return, we included some newly made northern Cheyenne specimens of beadwork for the Denver Art Museum's collection, including a beaded lock of hair, carefully laid between layers of dried fragrant wild sage.

* * *

Mama and Eric Douglas are both gone now, but I like to think of them sitting side by side on comfortable clouds, and examining Cheyenne beadwork. And of Mama's inevitable disdain for something that did not meet her standards. "Sioux?" she is saying, or even worse, "Crow!"

Alice Marriott

EPILOGUE
The Plains Today

We have come to the end of our stories. Maybe, just maybe, you are wondering about the Plains Indians today? If so we would like to say a little about them.

The political, social, and economic situations among the Plains Indians are so unbelievably varied and complicated that, while one may have opinions about them, it is impossible to form or express any judgments. It will probably be years—if ever—before the puzzles are finally resolved.

Many Plains Indian tribes live today in approximately the same geographic areas they occupied during horseback days. Removal simply did not work the same way with these seminomadic, hunting and fighting people as it did with the more docile horticultural tribes of the east.

All Indians in the United States are voting citizens. None is "a ward of the government." There are restricted lands—restricted in terms of sale or leasing but no "restricted Indians." In some states there are reservation areas; in others, trust lands are set aside for tribal or individual use. Each tribe theoretically controls the use of its own lands, although actual determinations are often made by the United States Bureau of Indian Affairs of the Department of the Interior.

Unfair this situation, maybe; complicated it undoubtedly is. The legal reelings and writhings and fainting in coils consequent to a series

of treaties that began in the sixteenth century and continued almost to
the end of the nineteenth are fearful to behold. No wonder most Indians have withdrawn into the safe seclusion of nonexistent wardship in
order to resist—to a remarkable degree—all attempts to make anything of them but what they have always been. *Indians.*

The Indian of today is a different Indian from the Indian of even a
few years ago, as we are different in attitudes and experiences from
our own parents and grandparents. A young Indian does not want to
submerge his identity in the non-Indian world; instead, he has a
greater awareness of his identity as an Indian, and wishes to impress
others with that awareness and its resulting attitudes. He wants to
blend some of the old with some of the new to gain a better, or at least
a different, way to live. The young Indian clings to his own tribal
identity, but he is becoming increasingly aware of the value of Pan-Indianism. The sum total of the strength of a minority group will always
be greater than the strength of any one segment of the group.

Pan-Indianism was called into action in the late 1960s when militant
Indians forcefully took over Alcatraz, the former federal prison in
San Francisco Bay, demanding that it become an educational insti-
tute for Indians. This attempt failed. In the early 1970s, to continue to
draw attention to their militant protests against the Government, the
Indians took over the town of Wounded Knee on the Pine Ridge reservation of the Sioux in South Dakota, where in the late 1800s the great
Indian massacre took place. Many arrests were made and the issues
were reported on television. Some months later in protest of their
treatment at Wounded Knee a group of Indians went to Washington,
D.C., and took possession of the Bureau of Indian Affairs. Much dam-
age was done to the building and furnishings and many great Indian
art works were ruined or stolen. Each of these tragedies is an example
of the same forces. All had to include Plains Indians in order to
succeed. Leadership came, in part, from the southern Plains, but it
took the Sioux of the northern Plains to drive the final point home.
As in the late 1800s the great Siouan-speaking block of the north
will again be the last stronghold of Plains Indians' resistance,
because there tribal differences are more easily overcome than in the
south.

Attempts to stage another Wounded Knee in Oklahoma, for example, have failed to date. The diversity of tribes in language and histo-
ries, no matter how acculturated their individual members may be, will

make tribal affiliation come before Pan-Indianism. This is not to say that the southern Plains does not have Pan-Indianism; because it does. Tribes work together in intertribal councils, and social events, such as the American Indian Exposition, held each summer in Anadarko, Oklahoma. But the southern Plains never were nor never will be as homogeneous as the northern Plains. And a Wounded Knee had to have Pan-Indians even partially to succeed.

The new Indian will struggle differently for his identity from the way in which his grandfather fought for his. But the young Indian will equip himself, not with a lance and a war bonnet, but with an education. There will be many Indian lawyers in the future, as well as doctors, engineers, businessmen, and members of other trades and professions. Indians will once again, after more than four centuries, have the know-how for survival.

But let us not forget Alcatraz, Wounded Knee, Washington, and other future battlefields. If Indians, especially Plains Indians, are to remain themselves, they must have symbols and rallying points, like everyone else. A man in battle used to drive his spear into the ground through the trailers of his war bonnet. Once he had set his spear, only death or a companion as brave as he, could release him. The Plains Indians of today, particularly, have set their spears, and they may not pull them from the ground.

BIBLIOGRAPHY

BARBEAU, MARIUS. *Indian Days on the Western Prairies.* Anthropological Series No. 46, Bulletin No. 163, Ottawa, Canada: National Museum of Canada, 1960.

BASS, ALTHEA. *The Arapaho Way.* New York, New York: Clarkson N. Potter, Inc., 1966.

BATTEY, THOMAS C. *The Life and Adventures of a Quaker Among the Indians.* Introduction by Alice Marriott, Norman, Oklahoma: University of Oklahoma Press, 1968.

BETZINEZ, JASON, with W. S. NYE. *I Fought with Geronimo.* Harrisburg, Pennsylvania: The Stackpole Company, 1959.

BRANCH, E. DOUGLAS. *The Hunting of the Buffalo.* Lincoln, Nebraska: University of Nebraska, 1962.

BRILL, CHARLES J. *Conquest of the Southern Plains.* Oklahoma City, Oklahoma: Golden Saga Publishers, 1938.

BROWN, JOSEPH EPES (Recorded and edited). *The Sacred Pipe: Black Elk's Account of the Seven Rites of the Ogalala Sioux.* Norman, Oklahoma: University of Oklahoma Press, 1953.

CARROLL, JOHN M. *Buffalo Soldiers West.* Fort Collins, Colorado: The Old Army Press, 1971.

CATLIN, GEORGE. *North American Indians.* Vols. I and II. London, England: 1851.

COHE. Commentary by E. Adamson Hoebell and Karen Daniels Petersen. *A Cheyenne Sketchbook.* Norman, Oklahoma: University of Oklahoma Press, 1964.

CORWIN, HUGH D. *The Kiowa Indians.* Lawton, Oklahoma: Privately Published, 1958.

DENIG, EDWIN THOMPSON. Edited by JOHN C. EWERS. *Of the Crow Nation.* Anthropological Paper, No. 33, Bureau of American Ethnology, Bulletin 151, pp 1-74, pls 1-6, Washington, D.C.: Government Printing Office, 1953.

DORSEY, GEORGE A. *The Cheyenne.* Anthropological Series Vol. IX, No. 2, Publication 103, Chicago, Illinois: Field Columbian Museum, 1905.
 The Ponca Sun Dance. Anthropological Series Vol. VII, No. 2, Publication 102, Chicago, Illinois: Field Columbian Museum, 1905.

EASTMAN, ELAINE GOODALE. *Pratt: The Red Man's Moses.* Norman, Oklahoma: University of Oklahoma Press, 1935.

EWERS, JOHN C. *The Horse in Blackfoot Indian Culture.* Smithsonian Institution, Bureau of American Ethnology Bulletin 159, Washington, D.C.: Government Printing Office, 1955.
 The Blackfeet. Norman, Oklahoma: University of Oklahoma Press, 1958.
 Indian Life on the Upper Missouri. Norman, Oklahoma: University of Oklahoma Press, 1968.

FAST, HOWARD. *The Last Frontier.* New York, New York: New American Library, 1941.

GREGG, ELINOR D. *The Indians and the Nurse.* Norman, Oklahoma: University of Oklahoma Press, 1965.

GREGG, JOSIAH. Edited by Max L. Moorhead. *Commerce of the Prairies.* Norman, Oklahoma: University of Oklahoma Press, 1954.

GRINNELL, GEORGE BIRD. *The Fighting Cheyennes.* Norman, Oklahoma: University of Oklahoma Press, 1956.
 By Cheyenne Campfires. New Haven, Connecticut: Yale University Press, 1962.
 The Cheyenne Indians—Their History and Way of Life. Vols. I and II. New York, New York: Cooper Square, Inc. 1962.

HAMILTON, W. T. *My Sixty Years on the Plains.* Norman, Oklahoma: University of Oklahoma Press, 1960.

HOEBEL, E. ADAMSON. *The Cheyennes: Indians of the Great Plains.* Case Studies in Cultural Anthropology, University of Minnesota, New York, New York: Holt-Dryden, 1960.

HOIG, STAN. *The Sand Creek Massacre.* Norman, Oklahoma: University of Oklahoma Press, 1961.

HOWARD, JAMES H. *Known Village Sites of the Ponca.* Plains Anthropologist Journal of the Plains Conference, 1970.

HYDE, GEORGE E. *A Sioux Chronicle.* Norman, Oklahoma: University of Oklahoma Press, 1956.
 Indian of the High Plains. Norman, Oklahoma: University of Oklahoma Press, 1959.

JONES, DOUGLAS C. *The Treaty of Medicine Lodge.* Norman, Oklahoma: University of Oklahoma Press, 1966.

KRAENZEL, CARL FREDERICK. *The Great Plains.* Norman, Oklahoma: University of Oklahoma Press, 1955.

KNIGHT, OLIVER. *Following the Indian Wars.* Norman, Oklahoma: University of Oklahoma Press, 1960.

LECKIE, WILLIAM H. *The Buffalo Soldiers: A Narrative of the Negro Cavalry in the West.* Norman, Oklahoma: University of Oklahoma Press, 1967.

LEE, NELSON (Narrator). *Three Years Among the Comanches: The Narrative of Nelson Lee, the Texas Ranger.* Norman, Oklahoma: University of Oklahoma Press, 1957.

LESSER, ALEXANDER. *The Pawnee Ghost Dance Hand Game.* Columbia University Contribution to Anthropology, XVI. New York, New York: Columbia University Press, 1933.

LLEWELLYN, K. N., and E. ADAMSON HOEBEL. *The Cheyenne Way.* Norman, Oklahoma: University of Oklahoma Press, 1941.

LOWIE, ROBERT H. *The Crow Indians.* New York, New York: Farrar & Rinehart, Inc., 1935.

  Indians of the Plains. Anthropological Handbook No. 1, The American Museum of Natural History. New York, New York: McGraw-Hill Book Co., Inc., 1954.

McCALLUM, HENRY D. and FRANCES. *The Wire That Fenced the West.* Norman, Oklahoma: University of Oklahoma Press, 1965.

McKENNEY, THOMAS L. and JAMES HALL. (New edition edited by Frederick Webb Hodge). *The Indian Tribes of North America.* Vols. I, II, III. Edinburgh, England: John Grant, 1933.

MARRIOTT, ALICE. *Winter-Telling Stories.* New York, New York: Thomas Y. Crowell Company, 1947.

  Indians on Horseback. Eau Claire, Wisconsin: Cadmus Books, E. M. Hale and Company, 1948.

  The Ten Grandmothers. Norman, Oklahoma. University of Oklahoma Press, 1957.

  Saynday's People. Lincoln, Nebraska: University of Nebraska Press, 1963. (Combines *Winter-Telling Stories* and *Indians on Horseback.*)

  Indian Annie: Kiowa Captive. New York, New York: David McKay Company, Inc., 1965.

  The Black Stone Knife. New York, New York. Archway Paperbacks, Washington Square Press, Inc. (1967 edition).

  Kiowa Years. Anthropology Curriculum Study Project of the American Anthropological Association. New York, New York: Macmillan & Co., Inc., 1967.

MARRIOTT, ALICE and CAROL K. RACHLIN. *American Indian Mythology.* New York, New York: Thomas Y. Crowell Co., 1968.

  Peyote. New York, New York: Thomas Y. Crowell Co., 1971.

MATHEWS, JOHN JOSEPH. *The Osages.* Norman, Oklahoma: University of Oklahoma Press, 1962.

MAYHALL, MILDRED P. *The Kiowas.* Norman, Oklahoma: University of Oklahoma Press, 1962.

MORROW, MABLE. *Indian Rawhide.* Norman, Oklahoma: University of Oklahoma Press, 1975.

MOONEY, JAMES. *The Ghost-Dance Religion.* Bureau of American Ethnology—Fourteenth Annual Report, Smithsonian Institution, 1892-1893, Part 2, Washington, D.C.: Government Printing Office, 1896.

MOORHEAD, MAX L. *The Apache Frontier: Jacob Ugarte & Spanish-Indian Relations in Northern New Spain 1769-1791.* Norman, Oklahoma: University of Oklahoma Press, 1968.

NABOKOV, PETER. *Two Leggings: The Making of a Crow Warrior.* Based on a field manuscript by William Wildschut for the Museum of the American Indian, Heye Foundation. New York, New York: Thomas Y. Crowell Co., 1967.

NYE, WILBUR STURTEVANT. *Carbine & Lance.* Norman, Oklahoma. University of Oklahoma Press, 1942.
    Bad Medicine & Good. Norman, Oklahoma: University of Oklahoma Press, 1962.
    Plains Indian Raiders. Norman, Oklahoma: University of Oklahoma Press, 1968.

PENNEY, GRACE JACKSON. *Tales of the Cheyenne.* Cambridge, Mass.: The Riverside Press, 1953.

PRATT, RICHARD HENRY (Edited with and Introduction by Robert M. Utley). *Battlefield and Classroom.* New Haven, Connecticut: Yale University Press, 1964.

RISTER, CARL COKE. *Southern Plainsmen.* Norman, Oklahoma: University of Oklahoma Press, 1938.

ROE, FRANK GILBERT. *The Indian and the Horse.* Norman, Oklahoma: University of Oklahoma Press, 1955.

RYDEN, HOPE. *America's Last Wild Horses.* New York, New York: E. P. Dutton & Co., Inc., 1970.

SANDOZ, MARI. *Cheyenne Autumn.* New York, New York: McGraw-Hill Co., 1953.

SCHULTZ, J. W. *My Life as an Indian.* New York, New York: A Premier Book, Fawcett World Library, 1956.
    Blackfeet and Buffalo. (Edited with an Introduction by Keith C. Steele.) Norman, Oklahoma: University of Oklahoma Press, 1962.

SEGER, JOHN H. (Edited by W. S. Campbell.) *Early Days Among the Cheyenne and Arapaho Indians.* Norman, Oklahoma: University of Oklahoma Press, 1956.

SIMPSON, GEORGE GAYLORD. *Horses.* The Natural History Library, Garden City, New York: American Museum of Natural History, A Doubleday Anchor Book, 1961.

SPIER, LESLIE. *The Sun Dance of the Plains Indians.* Anthropological Papers of the American Museum of Natural History, Volume XVI, Part VII, New York, New York: American Museum of Natural History, 1921.

STANDS IN TIMBER, JOHN, and MARGOT LIBERTY. *Cheyenne Memories.* New Haven, Connecticut: Yale University Press, 1967.

SWANTON, JOHN R. *The Indian Tribes of North America.* Bureau of American Ethnology Bulletin 145, Washington, D.C.: Government Printing Office, 1953.

TILGHMAN, ZOE A. *Quanah.* Oklahoma City, Oklahoma: Harlow Publishing Corporation, 1938.

TRENHOLM, VIRGINIA COLE. *The Arapahoes.* Norman, Oklahoma: University of Oklahoma Press, 1970.

WALLACE, ERNEST, and E. ADAMSON HOEBEL. *The Comanche.* Norman, Oklahoma: University of Oklahoma Press, 1952.

WELTFISH, GENE. *The Lost Universe.* New York, New York: Basic Books Inc., 1965.

WHITE, E. E. (Introduction by Edward Everett Dale). *Experiences of a Special Indian Agent.* Norman, Oklahoma: University of Oklahoma Press, 1965.

WISSLER, CLARK. *North American Indians of the Plains.* Handbook series No. 1, American Museum of Natural History, Lancaster, Pa.: Lancaster Press, Inc., 1927.

VOGEL, VIRGIL J. *American Indian Medicine.* Norman, Oklahoma: University of Oklahoma Press, 1970.

BIBLIOGRAPHY FOR MAP

KROEBER, A. L. *Cultural and Natural Areas of Native America.* Berkeley, Calif.: University of California Press, 1953.

SWANTON, JOHN R. *The Indian Tribes of North America.* Smithsonian Institution, Bureau of American Ethnology, Bulletin 145, Washington, D.C. 1953.

Handbook of American Indians, Bureau of American Ethnology, Bulletin 30, parts 1 and 2, 1906.